TERMINATOR
GENISYS

RESETTING THE FUTURE

TERMINATOR
GENISYS

RESETTING THE FUTURE

INSIDE THE CREATION OF THE EPIC NEW TERMINATOR SAGA

WRITTEN BY DAVID S. COHEN
FOREWORD BY ARNOLD SCHWARZENEGGER

INSIGHT  EDITIONS

San Rafael, California

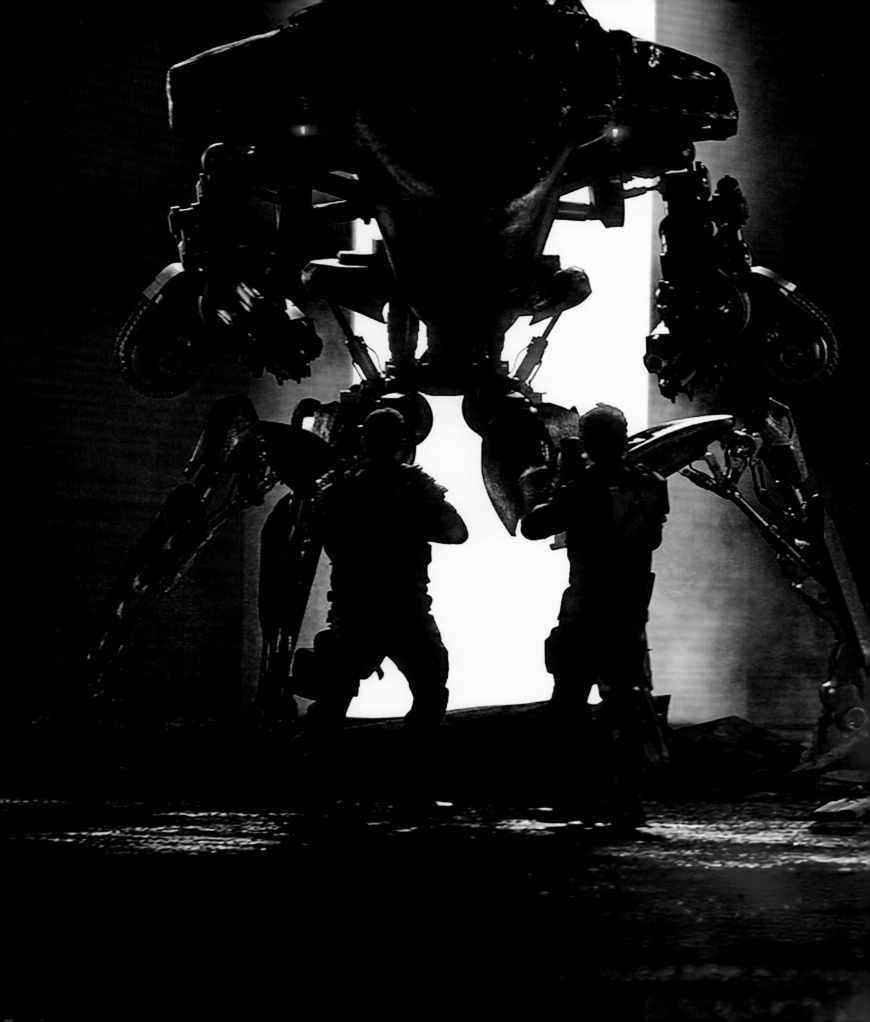

CONTENTS

FOREWORD
BY ARNOLD SCHWARZENEGGER

"I'LL BE BACK." The first time I read that line, I didn't even want to say it. I thought that machines wouldn't use contractions, but *The Terminator* was James Cameron's masterpiece, and he set me straight. I had no idea that "I'll be back" would become one of the most quoted film lines of all time, or that three decades later, it would be somewhat prophetic.

I am thrilled to be playing this iconic character once again in *Terminator Genisys*. However, while Guardian may be the same model of terminator I played thirty years ago, he is a very different character. In each successive Terminator movie, I have always insisted that we give the fans something new and exciting, and not just tread old ground. In *Terminator Genisys*, the character I play is a natural progression of an idea that we first explored in *Terminator 2: Judgment Day*: All terminators have a CPU that is able to learn and modify their behavior so that they can seem more human. Guardian has been around for decades, protecting the young Sarah Connor, and so he has learned to be more human than other terminators, and he has functioned almost as a father figure for her. That does not mean that he is perfect at replicating human behavior, though, and that gives us a lot of opportunity for humorous and emotional moments in this movie, as well as the groundbreaking action that fans demand from a Terminator film.

This book explores the creation of *Terminator Genisys* and all the incredible work that went into bringing it to the screen, from the thrilling screenplay by Laeta Kalogridis and Patrick Lussier to Alan Taylor's excellent direction and the tireless producing skills of David Ellison and Dana Goldberg. It also highlights the work of my incredible co-stars, including Emilia Clarke, Jai Courtney, and Jason Clarke, along with J. K. Simmons and the entire production team who brought the movie to life.

This book captures all the fun and excitement of creating this fantastic new movie in the Terminator saga, and I hope you enjoy the experience as much as I did. Over thirty years after starring in the original film, it is still a huge thrill to play the Terminator, especially when there are so many new dimensions to the character. I know my fans have been waiting a long time for *Terminator Genisys*, and I'm so happy to once again be able to fulfill my promise. I am back.

PART **1** | RISING TO THE CAUSE (RESET & SCRIPT)

01

THE RESET

"THE MACHINES ROSE FROM THE ASHES OF THE NUCLEAR FIRE. THEIR WAR TO EXTERMINATE MANKIND HAD RAGED FOR DECADES, BUT THE FINAL BATTLE WOULD NOT BE FOUGHT IN THE FUTURE. IT WOULD BE FOUGHT HERE IN OUR PRESENT. TONIGHT . . . "

—Opening title card, *The Terminator*

"WHY NOW?"

That was the question looming over David Ellison and Dana Goldberg in the spring of 2011 as they pondered whether to go after the rights to the Terminator franchise.

Ellison, CEO of film production company Skydance Productions, and Goldberg, Skydance's chief creative officer, were fans of the Terminator saga but, most of all, fans of the first two films, which had been directed by James Cameron. Those films had entered the culture—Who doesn't associate Schwarzenegger with the line "I'll be back"?—but they had been born of Cold War terrors, the threat of nuclear annihilation, and the fear that mankind's own technology bore the seeds of our species' destruction.

The Terminator universe imagined a future war between humankind and machines, with the machines turning humans' nuclear arsenals against them. "James Cameron made two of the best science-fiction films ever," says Ellison. Goldberg adds: "David and I sort of prayed at the altar of *The Terminator* and *Terminator 2: Judgment Day*." The power of *The Terminator* was undeniable, and after three decades it has remained a fan favorite. The cultural terrors that inspired it, though, were the terrors of the baby boom generation. Ellison and Goldberg had to find a reason to make a new Terminator in the 2010s. They loved Cameron's films too much to deliver a story that failed to resonate like the original. Therefore, they needed to explore concepts that would hit the same nerves among the children and grandchildren of the boomers.

After studying Cameron's Terminator pictures, they found their answer was no farther away than their desks and pockets: "The machines are everywhere," says Goldberg. "We are all connected 24/7, and we're connected by choice, not because Skynet is forcing us to be connected. It's sort of the ultimate dream for the machines." What if a new Terminator movie explored not defense tech but consumer tech? With jitters over privacy, tracking, and the abuse of personal data, it wasn't hard to imagine that humankind could be threatened

OPPOSITE: The Time Displacement Device is one of the many elements of the Terminator franchise that will be seen for the first time in *Terminator Genisys*.

not by a defense algorithm but by the gadgets we stand in long lines to buy and the cloud software that powers them. What if the menace threatening humanity was an app, maybe with a catchy name like Genisys?

——— <> ———

As Ellison and Goldberg planned their new approach to a Terminator film, they studied the creative and business history of the franchise. Though *The Terminator* is now a genre classic, it began as a low-budget science-fiction action picture from a young, unknown husband-and-wife team, James Cameron and Gale Anne Hurd. They emerged from

"THE TERMINATOR TURNED OUT TO BE ROMANTIC, THRILLING, INDELIBLE—AND WILDLY SUCCESSFUL."

producer Roger Corman's B-movie factory with lots of hands-on experience in production but little to recommend them as director and producer. Cameron's only feature directing credit was *Piranha II: The Spawning*; Hurd, his producer and cowriter, had no credits in either post. But they had a good script—good enough, anyway, to get the film funded if a big name star would sign on to reassure financiers.

They found their man in Arnold Schwarzenegger, a former Mr. Olympia whose only major leading role was in 1982's *Conan the Barbarian*. They let it be known that Schwarzenegger was to play the hero, a soldier from the future. That satisfied potential financiers, but Cameron, Hurd, and Schwarzenegger secretly had other plans. Eventually, in a canny bit of subterfuge, they let it be known that Schwarzenegger had asked to change parts and play the eponymous role, a lethal cyborg from the future known as a terminator.

The backers of *The Terminator* thought they were making a disposable exploitation film, but Cameron and Hurd had bigger ideas. Their story had a propulsive simplicity. At the end of an apocalyptic future war between mankind and machines, with humanity about to win, the machines had sent a lethal robot "infiltration unit," or terminator, to the past to kill the mother of John Connor, the resistance leader who had led the humans to victory and so prevent him from ever being born. Discovering the machines' gambit, Connor sent back a single solder,

OPPOSITE TOP: A new T-800 is deployed from Skynet's T-800 assembly room. OPPOSITE BOTTOM: The T-800 makes its way to the Time Displacement Device to be transported back to Los Angeles, circa 1984.

Kyle Reese, to stop the terminator and protect his mother, Sarah Connor. Sarah is revered in the future as the mother of humanity, the woman who recognized the threat of the machines and trained her son from birth for the war to come. But Reese finds not a warrior but a naïve waitress. In the extended chase that follows, the terminator survives every weapon Reese can throw at it. Before Reese dies fighting to save Sarah, they fall in love, and his death ultimately galvanizes Sarah, giving her the strength to destroy the terminator and prepare for the war to come. In the movie's coda, it's revealed that Sarah and Reese have conceived a child: John Connor.

The Terminator turned out to be romantic, thrilling, indelible—and wildly successful. It launched Cameron, Hurd, and Schwarzenegger into the filmmaking stratosphere. Seven years later, atop Hollywood's pinnacle,

ABOVE: The interior of Skynet's Time Displacement Device was conceived as a vast space not made for human access.

Cameron and Schwarzenegger reunited for a sequel, *Terminator 2: Judgment Day*. This time Schwarzenegger's cyborg was the good guy, programmed to protect Sarah from a shape-shifting "liquid metal" terminator. Linda Hamilton's now tough and world-weary Sarah became a sensation in her own right. *Terminator 2: Judgment Day* (aka *T2*) was far from low-budget, but it grossed over half a billion dollars. The public clearly loved this story and seemed ready for more.

But Cameron walked away from the franchise, moving on to *True Lies* with Schwarzenegger, then *Titanic*, and eventually *Avatar*. Ever since, the Terminator universe has tantalized producers. Following *T2*, the Terminator saga continued without Cameron with 2003's *Terminator 3: Rise of the Machines* and 2009's *Terminator: Salvation*. A TV series, *Terminator: The Sarah Connor Chronicles*,

also hit the small screen in 2008 with Lena Headey as the eponymous heroine. While these projects found an audience, they never quite entered the zeitgeist like Cameron's film, leaving a generation of fans craving more films that captured the spirit of the originals. And in that generation were people with the means and resolve to make those films, if they could only get the opportunity to do it. Among them were two siblings, David and Megan Ellison.

David, the elder, had founded film production company Skydance Productions in 2010 with the goal of building movie franchises and expansive cinematic universes. Within a few years, it had produced several hits based on pre-existing intellectual properties, including *True Grit* (a remake), *Mission Impossible: Ghost Protocol* (a sequel), and *World War Z* (from a bestselling book). Megan founded her own film company, Annapurna Productions,

in 2011, aiming to make auteur-driven pictures. Among its projects were three Oscar contenders: Paul Thomas Anderson's *The Master*, Kathryn Bigelow's *Zero Dark Thirty*, and Spike Jonze's riff on artificial intelligence, *Her*.

The rights to the Terminator franchise had come up for sale following the release of *Terminator 3: Rise of the Machines*, but David Ellison had missed the chance to buy them. Now, due to his sister's efforts, he had another chance.

Megan Ellison and Annapurna won a bidding war for the Terminator film rights in spring 2011. For a time, Annapurna considered producing a new Terminator film alone, but in late 2012, Megan Ellison reconsidered and asked her brother if Skydance would partner on the reset. "I said 'Look, I love this. We've always wanted to do this,'" says David Ellison. But the Ellisons wanted to create a

cohesive universe spanning all media, including films, comics, games, and more. "We couldn't build that world unless all of the rights could actually reside within one company," says David Ellison. Over the years, those rights had been sold off and divided among several companies. Megan and David Ellison agreed that Skydance should be the company to acquire them all and keep them under one roof. Consolidating those rights kept lawyers busy for months, but in early 2013, the task was done.

Once Skydance had the rights to the franchise, Ellison and Goldberg continued exploring options for revitalizing the saga. In the process, they grasped something simple yet essential about Cameron's two Terminator films: At heart, they are love stories.

"The first movie is dressed up as a horror film or action film, but it does not function without the line: 'I came

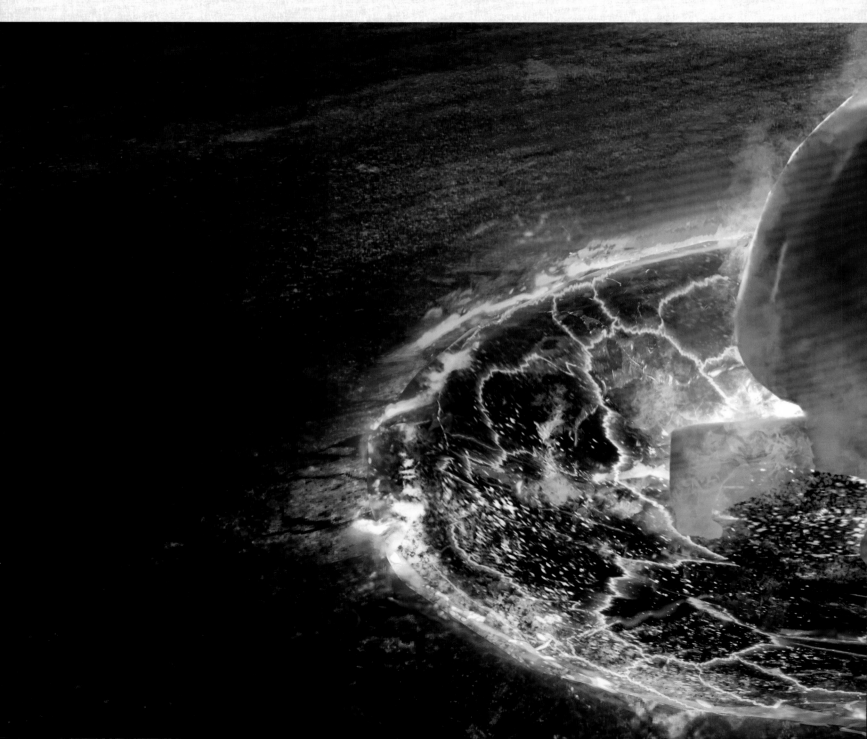

across time for you, Sarah,'" says Goldberg. "The second one is absolutely a father-son love story, the story of a family. The most memorable part of *T2*, for all of the incredible visual effects and chases, is the voiceover Sarah gives while she's watching Arnold with John Connor: 'He's the perfect father. He'll never hurt him. He'll never leave him. He'll always protect him.'"

Yes, any new Terminator film would need to have all the chases and action and cutting-edge visuals that a twenty-first-century Hollywood blockbuster can muster, and yes, it would deal with paranoid fears about technology, but it would need to have a love story at its core.

Skydance next needed someone to fashion a script from the broad concept Ellison and Goldberg had hammered out. Happily, they were already working with a writing team well-suited to the material: Laeta Kalogridis and Patrick Lussier. Kalogridis was an experienced action writer who, coincidentally, was a friend of James Cameron, having worked with him as a producer on *Avatar*. Lussier was a film editor turned writer-director whose credits included *My Bloody Valentine 3D* and

Drive Angry. The duo had been writing a science-fiction script for Skydance and had turned in a first draft that David Ellison and Goldberg had loved.

"I was very familiar with Patrick's work as an editor," says Ellison. "He has an incredible résumé and has edited some phenomenal movies. And Laeta was somebody I had wanted to work with for years, but every time I called her, she was simply not available. "From that moment we had our first creative meeting together, I knew I had found collaborative partners that I would want to work with for the rest of my career."

As happy as they were to be working with Skydance, taking on a new Terminator was another matter.

"I said no a few times," says Laeta, "out of respect for James Cameron, the universe he created." She also admits to being afraid she wouldn't live up to Cameron's storytelling abilities. But she relented after Cameron reassured her that he was comfortable with where Skydance meant to take the story. He did have one instruction for Kalogridis, though, and she took it to heart: "Make sure you write a great role for Arnold."

BELOW: The arrival of the T-800 in 1984 Los Angeles would have to be re-created in *Terminator Genisys*.

02

FACE-TO-FACE WITH THE TERMINATOR

FOR DAVID ELLISON, THE SKYDANCE TEAM, AND THE WRITERS, there was never a doubt: If they were going to make a new *Terminator* film, they wanted Arnold Schwarzenegger in it. "He is the terminator. I mean, you cannot make a Terminator movie without him," says Ellison. Goldberg adds: "We knew that if push came to shove, and he said 'No, I absolutely don't want to revisit this,' then we'd have to figure out a way. But we always wanted Arnold to be in this movie not in a scene or two but in a significant fashion."

Schwarzenegger had been unavailable for *Terminator: Salvation*, as he was governor of California at the time. But by 2013 he had retired from politics and returned to acting. Getting him on board seemed possible, although he was now three decades older than when he first appeared in the original Terminator movie. To bring him back would mean either restoring his youthful appearance through some combination of makeup and visual effects or explaining why there should be an older-looking terminator. But, in fact, Cameron had opened the door to an aging terminator all the way back in the first film. As Kyle Reese explains to Sarah about the T-800: "The Terminator's an infiltration unit: part man, part machine. Underneath, it's a hyperalloy combat chassis—micro processor-controlled, fully armored. Very tough. But outside, it's living human tissue—flesh, skin, hair, blood—grown for the cyborgs . . ." If a T-800 had living skin and flesh, that flesh could age.

> **"HE BASICALLY SAID, 'THE BAR HAS BEEN SET PRETTY HIGH, AND I EXPECT YOU TO MEET IT IN ORDER FOR ME TO BE REALLY EXCITED ABOUT DOING THIS.'"**

So the Skydance team decided not to run away from Schwarzenegger's age. "Own it," says Goldberg. "It's a significant part of this film, the idea of a terminator aging, a terminator changing."

Ellison reached out to Schwarzenegger's representatives, who quickly called back to arrange a breakfast meeting for the next morning at Marmalade Cafe, a relaxed spot in

RIGHT: For David Ellison and the team at Skydance, it was hard to imagine making a Terminator film without Arnold Schwarzenegger.

Malibu. "I think it was a Saturday," says Ellison, "8:30 a.m. I got there about fifteen minutes early because I didn't want to be late." Ellison told him about the plans for a franchise reset, and the meeting ended with Schwarzenegger expressing interest—but not making a firm commitment, since he couldn't yet read a script.

That began a process of courting the legendary star, assuring him that the story, script, and overall production would meet his standards. Goldberg had her own sit-down with Schwarzenegger at Toscana, a Brentwood gathering spot for entertainment moguls. It was her first time meeting him, and she arrived nervous, but he quickly put her at ease. There wasn't yet a draft of the script, but Schwarzenegger was encouraging, remembers Goldberg. "He basically said, 'The bar has been set pretty high, and I expect you to meet it in order for me to be really excited about doing this.'" But he was clear: If they did meet that bar, he'd be interested.

OPPOSITE TOP: A hoodie adds just a touch of softness to Guardian's menacing look. OPPOSITE BOTTOM: Schwarzenegger on set with David Ellison and Dana Goldberg. LEFT: Schwarzenegger with David Ellison on the set of *Terminator Genisys*. BELOW: Arnold Schwarzenegger has always added humanity to his Terminator characters.

03

WRITING
THE SCRIPT

AS KALOGRIDIS AND LUSSIER PREPARED to pitch their take on a Terminator reset, there was broad agreement on some ground rules. As it would harken back to *The Terminator* and *T2*, this Terminator universe would include Sarah Connor, Kyle Reese, John Connor, and some version of Schwarzenegger's T-800, the core characters of Cameron's original Terminator universe.

Kalogridis shared Ellison and Goldberg's affection for those films and wanted to write a story that lived squarely within that mythology. "For me, the most interesting characters in the franchise were always the ones in the first two movies," she says. With time having passed since Cameron's original vision, she and Lussier were also interested in the idea of an evolved machine that had lived among humans. They adopted an idea from *T2* that was cut from the theatrical version and later reinstated for a special extended edition of the film: a "learning chip" installed in the T-800 that allows it to assimilate and adapt to what's happening around it, making it a more efficient infiltration unit. That opened the door to a cyborg that was evolving in response to human society.

In fact, while the Terminator reset would bring back the original central characters, they would all be different from their incarnations in the earlier films. There would be a twist.

The original film had touched on a profound fear of the baby boomer generation: nuclear annihilation. In the early 1980s, says Kalogridis, "that's what was terrifying about technology." She and Lussier agreed that the risk of nuclear war no longer inspired the same technophobia, but people today do hold deep fears about the degree to which technology has become entwined in their lives. In the twenty-first century, we don't fear that we'll be destroyed by a defense algorithm gone rogue, but the idea of our smartphones turning against us is horrifying.

Lussier observes that the Terminator mythos has always been a Frankenstein story: "We create Skynet to take care of us, to solve human error, to protect us. But it has to work for us. If Skynet is not our bitch, it must be destroyed." In *T2*, it was established that Skynet attacked only after humans tried to turn it off.

RIGHT: *Terminator Genisys* gives audiences a vision of a world ruled by Skynet.

Schwarzenegger's prospective return helped Kalogridis and Lussier shape a narrative they call the *Unforgiven* version of a Terminator story. Just as Clint Eastwood's revisionist western exploited his own history as "The Man With No Name," their script would exploit Schwarzenegger's history as the terminator. He would play a cyborg again, but cyborgs aren't what they used to be. Technology has evolved, and that

"THERE'S A QUESTION THAT IS ALWAYS AT THE HEART OF ALL TERMINATOR MOVIES. WHERE DOES THE HUMANITY LIE?"

evolution would be central to the story in a way that would nod to Schwarzenegger's own off-camera evolution. "It was, 'How do we create a story around the thing that has evolved in our lives?'" Kalogridis says. "As an audience member, I don't want to see a CG version of Arnold in the last few minutes of a movie. I want to see the evolution. I want to see change, and because he is the same actor—older—he represents that."

Kalogridis and Lussier met with Ellison and Goldberg in January 2013 and pitched their ideas for the story. All the scenes they pitched in that meeting made it into their final script, among them the idea that a terminator, played by Schwarzenegger, would come back in time to the 1970s and save Sarah long before Kyle Reese appeared. That terminator, "Guardian," would end up raising her from age nine. Instead of finding the everywoman waitress of the original movie, Reese would find a find a warrior but one not very comfortable among people and not particularly impressed with Reese. So the love story between them would have an entirely different arc. "When you slap up against someone who is openly rejecting you, I think that's a very different dynamic," says Kalogridis.

Kalogridis and Lussier also pitched a new villain, the T-3000, who represents the union of man and machine, a dark version of the "singularity," the moment when artificial intelligence exceeds human intelligence, posited by such futurists as Ray Kurzweil. Both storywise and visually, the T-3000 would go beyond the shape-shifting "liquid metal"

T-1000 of *T2*. It, too, would be a shape-shifter, but instead of liquid, it would be made of tiny "nanocytes" that could rearrange themselves at will. The step forward, though, was that while the T-1000 was still simply a robot, a weapon programmed to kill, the T-3000 nanocytes would be able to merge with a human body. The danger of Skynet and the machines in the original Terminator films was that the machines might annihilate humankind. The new danger would be that the machines would assimilate humans—that humans would become simply another kind of networked device, all subject to the will of Skynet.

It's not entirely fantasy. Kalogridis observes that with contemporary society facing the imminent prospect of humans getting technological implants, where is the line between machine and man? When do you cease to be human? It was a topic Skydance felt needed to be in the film. "There's a question that is always at the heart of all Terminator movies," says Dana Goldberg. "Where does the humanity lie? Can a machine actually have a version of humanity? If you don't have that emotional core, the movie

will be entertaining, but, frankly, it won't be special."

The new script would not begin with the terminator's arrival in 1984, as the original film had, but it would introduce the audience to Kyle Reese as a soldier in the future and his relationship with John, who is Reese's biological son but is also his father figure. (Time travel can play havoc with family relationships that way.)

In scenes described but never seen in *The Terminator*, Connor and his forces discover Skynet has used a Time Displacement Device, or TDD, to send a T-800 back to kill Sarah. They use the same TDD to send Reese to protect her. Then the action shifts to 1984, when Sarah, Reese, and Guardian team up to battle the T-800 sent to kill Sarah and a shape-shifting T-1000 sent to intercept Kyle. Once the T-3000 appears, Reese and Sarah use a TDD that Guardian has assembled to jump forward in time to 2017, hoping to prevent the activation of Skynet. But Guardian has to remain and spends thirty-three more years among humans, preparing for Reese and Sarah's arrival in the future. So when they begin their showdown with the T-3000 and Skynet, Guardian has

ABOVE: Post-apocalyptic Los Angeles is featured in the early scenes of *Terminator Genisys*.

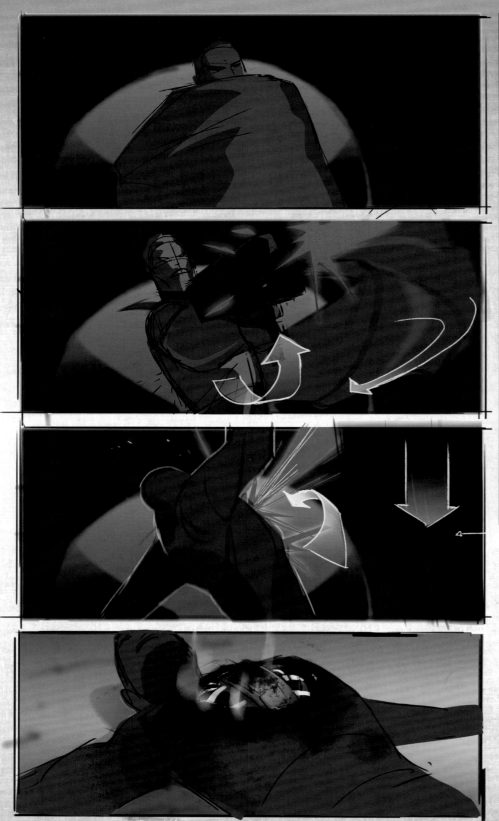

aged some forty years from when he first appeared, though his robotic innards are still functioning—more or less. "He's not a rust bucket," says director Alan Taylor, who would later be hired to helm *Terminator Genisys*, "but he's showing signs of wear and tear. It has an emotional impact on him and the characters around him."

That idea appealed to Schwarzenegger. "He encouraged the idea that this is the terminator with wrinkles, not the sleek version it was when he was younger," says Lussier. "This is a terminator with mileage."

Kalogridis and Lussier officially got the script assignment in January and set to work with Ellison and Goldberg to create a first draft. They would gather in the writers' office, where the walls were covered in whiteboards. Says Ellison, "We were just throwing the story up on the boards in the room and seeing what worked and what didn't work, and when something didn't work, we would pull it down and rework it. Patrick and Laeta would write twenty pages at a time. We would then give notes until we fundamentally had something we were happy with." That went on for about

six months until they had what they came to call "The July Draft," which was more or less the story that was filmed and was finished enough to show studios, directors, and actors.

The foursome of Ellison, Goldberg, Kalogridis, and Lussier became Skydance's brain trust not just for *Terminator Genisys* but for an entire planned trilogy. One thing they agreed on: A Terminator film shouldn't take place mostly in the apocalyptic post–Judgment Day future or focus on the Future War between the machines and the humans. "We knew that we wanted a movie that lives in the world that *T2* did," says Ellison. "Terminator films take place in our world, where you understand and can relate to everything around you. If you set everything in a post-apocalyptic world, even if you win the war against the machines, you've ultimately lost, because all you've really won is a barren wasteland left from a nuclear holocaust, and it's not a victory in itself."

"We in no way wanted to do a direct remake of *The Terminator*," Ellison says, "because it's a phenomenal movie, and we by no means wanted to repeat or redo what has already been done perfectly, as both *The Terminator*

and *T2* were. We really wanted to create something that was completely standalone, so if you were a fan of *The Terminator*, you would love the films, and obviously there would be great Easter eggs in there for you. But if you'd never seen a Terminator movie before, this would play as *Terminator 1*. Because otherwise there was really no reason to move forward with making this movie."

Once Schwarzenegger read the script, he asked David Ellison to meet over breakfast again. "I want to talk through it," Schwarzenegger told him. Their meeting ran for hours, as Schwarzenegger went through the script point by point to get clarity about the story.

Ellison remembers Schwarzenegger saying he was impressed with the script's intelligence and agreed it was reminiscent of the first two Terminator films. "The breakfast ended with him saying, 'I can't wait to do the movie,'" says Ellison.

Paramount Pictures, which has first refusal on Skydance projects, also liked the script and agreed to make the film. But there was not even a director under contract. Nothing was designed. There was a lot of work to do.

ABOVE AND OPPOSITE: Concept art and a set of storyboards depict the scene where John Connor saves the young Kyle Reese from a terminator.

04
THE CHARACTERS

THE "RESET" CHARACTERS of *Terminator Genisys* follow in a tradition that stretches back to Greek drama: the reinvention of familiar characters but with a new twist. Just as ancient Athenians knew the myths portrayed onstage and could be shocked or delighted by how they were reinterpreted, so too modern audiences know the story of the innocent Sarah Connor, the warrior Kyle Reese, their subsequent love, and valiant fight against the terminator. Turning Sarah into the warrior and Reese into the innocent is a twist Euripides would have appreciated.

Creating a character is normally considered the job of the writer and actor in collaboration with the director. But in a film like *Terminator Genisys* where so much of the story is told visually, other crafts play a crucial role.

> "THE WAY THE LIGHT PLAYS ON AN ACTOR'S FACE CAN TOTALLY MAKE OR BREAK THE WAY THAT THE CHARACTER IS INTERPRETED."

"The way the light plays on an actor's face can totally make or break the way that the character is interpreted," says cinematographer Kramer Morgenthau. "It's my job as a cinematographer to figure out a way to capture a face or a character that is both flattering and appropriate to the story and to the environments they're in—hopefully, the perfect blend of both. It's a collaboration between the actor, the cinematographer, hair, and makeup."

RIGHT: In 2017 San Francisco, Kyle Reese and Sarah Connor lead the fight against Skynet. OPPOSITE: Kyle Reese and John Connor charge into battle against the machines in the year 2029.

GUARDIAN

GUARDIAN, THE CYBORG THAT RAISED SARAH CONNOR, represents manmachine coexistence or at least "the possibility that we don't have to kill each other," says Lussier. For that reason, Kalogridis and Lussier regard Guardian as the pivotal figure in the planned trilogy.

Guardian is able to learn from his surroundings, and by the time the climax of *Terminator Genisys* arrives, it's an open question as to how much Guardian has been influenced by the humans he has lived among for forty years. If the overarching question raised by the *Terminator* franchise is "Can a machine have humanity?'" Guardian may eventually provide the answer.

Guardian has been running a long time. "For the first time we're seeing a terminator character who has a kind of vulnerability, because there are ways in which he is not fully functional, and he knows it," says Alan Taylor. "There's a kind of self-awareness and a kind of tragic quality that is new."

Guardian is seen at several ages. In flashbacks to Sarah's rescue, he appears identical to Schwarzenegger's original terminator. In 1984 he has already aged eleven years. In 2017 San Francisco, he has aged thirty-three more years—but he is better at blending in with the people around him. The idea was to create an eternal but not ageless character—Lussier calls him "A Flying Dutchman"—that has experienced humanity as an outsider.

In imagining Guardian, Kalogridis and Lussier created sequences—intended for flashback scenes but never shot for the film—of his life as Sarah's "Pops," the endearing nickname she uses for him throughout the movie. Entrusted with the protection and training of a little girl, the machine watched *Sesame Street* with her, read Dr. Spock, and treated parenting as a skill it could program itself for. He was single-minded in preparing

LEFT: As Guardian, Arnold Schwarzenegger plays a terminator that has protected Sarah since childhood. By the time the story begins, his flesh is aging, but he is "not obsolete." ABOVE: Drawings and photographs from Sarah's childhood show a paternal side to Guardian's character.

TOP: Guardian's efforts to fit in don't always work. ABOVE: Despite his quirks, Guardian is a cunning and lethal fighter, as he shows when he uses a teddy bear to smuggle a gun into a hospital. OPPOSITE: Storyboards depicting Guardian's fight with the T-1000.

her for battle. For years she begged for a tea party, and finally he gave her one—but they used the teacups for target practice. And as she moved into her teens, even more than most parents, he became a source of embarrassment and frustration, for Guardian can never entirely blend in, even though he was built as an "infiltration unit." These scenes of Guardian and Sarah's life helped the writers pin down the details of their personalities.

Does Guardian have genuine affection for Sarah? Does he have feelings at all? There are hints that he does. For example, he keeps little Sarah's drawings. "He didn't let go of them.

He kept them, I think, for a reason," says Kalogridis. Is that affection or something from a checklist on good parenting? "I, as a writer, like the fact that I don't entirely know," says Kalogridis. "I like not being sure about what's going on in his head."

Guardian may stand for hope, but the writers observe there's a paradox built into the very notion of a "good" cyborg programmed to protect. "We're comfortable as long as the technology is not in charge," says Kalogridis. "As long as it's a slave, we're fine."

CUT TO WIDE DUTCH
TILT OF GUARDIAN
HOLDING T-1000 DOWN
AS HIS LEGS KICK
+ STRUGGLE.

CUT TO LOW ANGLE
OF GUARDIAN,
ACID EATING UP
HIS ARM.
CONT. SPLASHING
FROM T-1000

REVEAL ENDO
HAND

SARAH CONNOR

"THE SARAH CONNOR FROM THE FIRST FILM was completely vulnerable," says Dana Goldberg. "She has no idea what's going on. She's just like the POV for the audience." Then, by the beginning of the events of *T2*, says Goldberg, "she's as close as a human can probably come to being a machine. There's a strength, too, that almost makes her crazy." Linda Hamilton excelled as both versions of the character.

The Sarah of *Terminator Genisys*, says Goldberg, is somewhere in between the Sarahs of *The Terminator* and *T2*. She saw the future and was warned what was coming, just like the Sarah of the first movie, but the warning came not in her twenties from her savior and lover but from the cyborg that dispatched the T-800 that killed her parents. That cyborg then not only trained her to be a fighter but warned her in detail of the events to come. So, like the Sarah of *T2*, she has lost loved ones and is physically prepared for a grim future. She's not on the edge of madness, as Sarah seems to be in *T2*, but she's socially stunted and uncomfortable with people. She even has more than a little in common with the original depiction of John Connor, who learned details about the coming war at his mother's feet.

"What I hope we ended up doing," says Kalogridis, "was taking a character that embodies all of this powerful warrior spirit and exploring what she would have been like if her life had been transformed in a different way. But the core of her is always the same. The core of her is sort of incorruptibly what's in the first two movies. I don't think it's possible to write her any other way." Even Sarah's costume puts her somewhere between Hamilton's performances. Costume designer Susan Matheson gave Sarah a look "where there's a toughness, but there's still a bit of a softness."

An audience used to the idea that Kyle Reese comes through time for the woman he loves and that the two of them "loved a lifetime's worth" in the few hours they had together

LEFT AND ABOVE: Emilia Clarke delivers a different take on the 1984 version of Sarah Connor—not the sweet naif played by Linda Hamilton in the original film, but a disciplined and sometimes difficult warrior woman.

is likely to find this new Sarah unexpectedly resistant to Reese's charms. "She spends a lot of time being a difficult person in our movie," says Taylor. "She gives people orders rather than connecting or relating to them. We're very aware that she hasn't had a normal relationship with a human being since she was nine years old."

Adds Taylor, "We know Sarah and Kyle are sort of meant for each other, but they're both very damaged, and it's not clear that they're actually going to be able to connect." Both have supportive but dysfunctional father figures: Guardian for Sarah and John Connor for Reese. "Those relationships are deeply screwed up," says Taylor. "These two people bring a lot of baggage with them."

Kalogridis notes that *The Terminator* starts out equally as Sarah and Reese's story, then becomes Sarah's story, and *T2* starts out as Sarah's story and becomes John's story. "This one is Reese's story at the beginning and becomes the story of a family at the end," she says.

From the start, the filmmakers knew that the actress who played Sarah would have to not only be able to handle the physical demands of the part but would have to be able to withstand comparison with Linda Hamilton and her iconic *T2* performance.

Emilia Clarke was on the producers' short list from the beginning. They had seen her as "Mother of Dragons" Daenerys Targaryen on the hit HBO series *Game of Thrones* and admired her portrayal. "She has the capacity to be powerful without becoming angry or harsh," says Alan Taylor, who'd directed her on *Game of Thrones*. "The other thing is she's just incredibly charismatic. She's got vulnerability, those beautiful big eyes of hers. Your heart goes out to her."

That charisma was crucial, since the Sarah in this version of the Terminator story is not fully socialized, as a psychologist might say. "She's a pain in the ass to be around," says Taylor. "But there's a tremendous likable vulnerability that comes through in Emilia, so even when she's yelling at you, you sense there is a richer soul underneath. That's one reason we were lucky to have her."

Nonetheless, Clarke still had to get through several rounds of auditions to win this much-in-demand role. Jai Courtney, who would be cast as Kyle Reese, was even flown in from Australia to read with her. "We can grasp the girl in the character," says Courtney of his costar. "But she can also turn on a dime and be this badass warrior woman. The script demands that we get a glimpse

BELOW: Costume concepts suggest both the tougher Sarah Connor of *Terminator 2* and, with her leather jacket, the original terminator himself.
OPPOSITE: Nonetheless, her look lets a softer and more vulnerable side come through at times.

T-800 guardian
takes young Sarah
by the Hand

of the child in all these characters. I think she plays that kind of contradiction—that dichotomy—really well."

Clarke had grown up with the Terminator pictures and says, "It was incredible to be considered to have the possibility of playing that much of a badass." Landing the role, she says, "was like birthday and Christmas all at once." Besides Sarah's ferocity and vulnerability, she also enjoyed the character's dry sense of humor.

"She grew up with a terminator for a dad, so I think there are a lot of jokes she kind of cultivated within herself without needing a response. So I think that sarcasm and dry humor are definitely within her repertoire. They give her that extra aggressive edge."

OPPOSITE: Storyboards for Guardian's rescue of young Sarah. ABOVE: In this timeline, Sarah is traumatized at a young age by the loss of her parents, with Guardian left to care for her. RIGHT: Schwarzenegger's T-800 was John Connor's father figure in *Terminator 2*; he takes on a similar role for Sarah in *Terminator Genisys*.

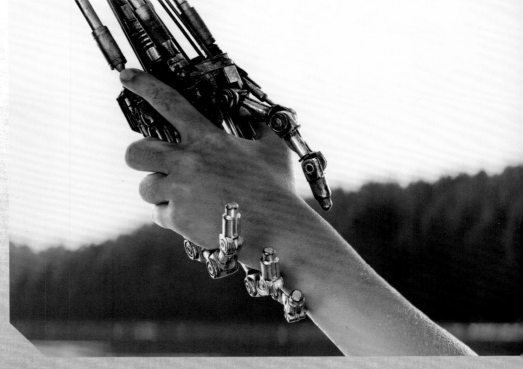

KYLE REESE

PART OF KALOGRIDIS AND LUSSIER'S PITCH TO SKYDANCE was the idea that Kyle Reese would be the focal character—"sort of a 'Gospel According to Reese,'" as Lussier puts it. For if, in *The Terminator*, Sarah Connor represents the audience, in *Terminator Genisys* Reese fulfills that function. Reese, like the audience, believes he knows what will happen after he arrives in Los Angeles circa 1984.

But once there, Sarah saves him, not the other way around, ironically delivering the iconic line "Come with me if you want to live" in the process. From that moment on, his story spins in radically new directions.

Sarah turns out to be his equal and far from the vulnerable naïf that he was told to expect. On the contrary, at times she can barely stand him. Then he learns that his mentor and idol, the savior of humanity, John Connor, is his own son with Sarah. "One series of events after another that puts him in a hurricane of 'What the fuck?'" as Lussier puts it.

So to face the fight in front of him, Reese must let go of his expectations, as must the audience. Before these mind-bending twists, the audience gets to see Reese's life before his fateful journey back to the twentieth century. In the opening 2029 sequence, says Lussier, "He has a life where he's a confidante of the general, the mastermind, the savior—John Connor." He's loyal, fierce, capable, dedicated, and absolutely hates machines.

Fight choreographer and co–stunt coordinator Melissa Stubbs worked on developing a fighting style for Reese that reflects the character. The key: survival instinct. "He's just an animal," says Stubbs. "He has brute strength, cunning, and he's very quick. He could survive anything and get out of any predicament."

Reese, Sarah, and Guardian form an oddly dysfunctional family. Pops is a robot that may not actually feel anything for Sarah. Reese hates machines and so is inclined

LEFT AND ABOVE: Jai Courtney's experience in action films proved perfect preparation for the physically demanding role of Kyle Reese.

KYLE REACHES FOR JOHN'S HAND, CAM TRACK W/ HAND

TILT UP TO REVEAL JOHN REACHING OUT HIS HAND TO KYLE.

TILT

to hate Pops. Pops is skeptical of Reese. Sarah trusts Pops but not Reese, and yet Reese and Sarah have a powerful attraction. Somehow they must meld together and become a functioning family if they are to defeat the cybernetic forces arrayed against them.

Finding the right actor to play Reese was a major concern, especially given fans' affection for Michael Biehn's definitive portrayal of the character in the original film. Fortunately, the filmmakers were able to find a charismatic actor to fill the role.

Terminator Genisys's director, producers, and stars are convinced Jai Courtney has the makings of a major movie star. Alan Taylor cites Courtney's intensity. Ellison says he is "incredibly charismatic, physically capable, and a strong actor." Kalogridis hails his "untapped potential." Audiences have previously seen him as a bad guy in *Divergent* and *Jack Reacher*, and Kalogridis affirms that "he can melt into the part, in much the same way that Michael Biehn could." Emilia Clarke marvels at the "vulnerabilities and

OPPOSITE TOP: Reese carries hazy memories of an alternative timeline, where Judgment Day never happened and he grew up in an intact home. This concept art shows the post-apocalyptic version of his family's house. OPPOSITE BOTTOM: Storyboards show the moment where young Kyle first meets John Connor, who, paradoxically, is actually Kyle's son. TOP AND LEFT: While Reese is a key figure in the future war with Skynet, he is unprepared for the fight he will face in 1984.

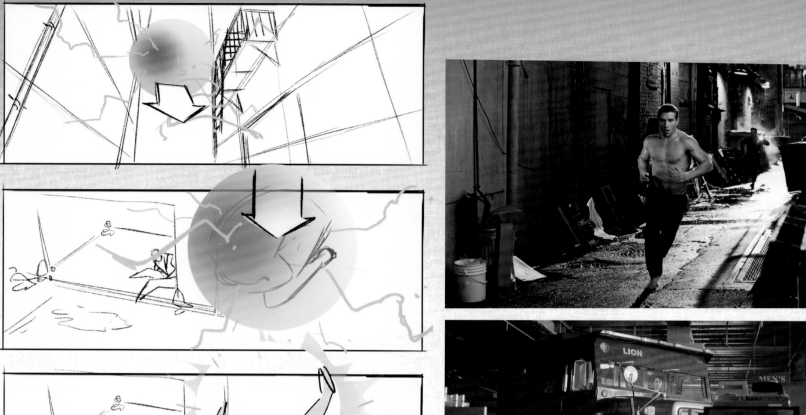
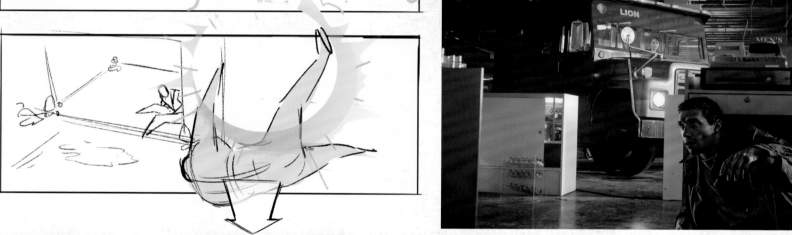

complexities that he has shown, whilst being a complete badass. I can hear girls all over the world swooning at his portrayal of Kyle Reese."

In auditions, Lussier recounts, "Jai was the one who completely understood this version of the character, understood the weight of what this character was before, while at the same time reinventing it." His "chemistry" script reading with Emilia Clarke sealed the deal.

As in the original film, Reese is a formidable warrior, but in *Terminator Genisys*, he's also a confused one. "It was kind of fun to be a fish out of water in that sense," says Courtney. "Not only is he in another time and place, but all the knowledge he was equipped with is essentially useless now, and he has to find a way to still accomplish the mission and keep Sarah and himself alive." Courtney brings something else to the role, too, says Taylor: "He's boyish and sometimes naive and sometimes overwhelmed by things around him. His character has a kind of sensitivity that is really important to capture, to explain not just why Sarah falls for him, but why he is uniquely able to handle the task that is given to him."

Kalogridis cites one more thing that made Courtney the right man for the job. "Physically, you could not ask for someone who's more ridiculously capable. I mean, it's *ridiculous*. You're hanging him upside down, you're throwing him off a building—he can do *anything*."

The cast gathered for the first time at a table reading, and there the new stars met Schwarzenegger. "You always have a bit of a pinch yourself moment," says Courtney, "when you're dealing with material of this nature or working with someone who is a hero of yours. And it was at that moment that I was like, 'Holy shit, here we are. I'm making a Terminator movie for real.'"

OPPOSITE TOP LEFT AND BOTTOM: Storyboards and concept art show that Reese's arrival in 1984 Los Angeles closely parallels the events of the original Terminator film— for a little while, at least. OPPOSITE TOP RIGHT: Kyle's flight from the T-1000 is assisted by the sudden arrival of Sarah Connor and Guardian in an armored truck. TOP: Concept art shows Kyle and Sarah fighting the T-1000 while escaping through the streets of downtown Los Angeles. ABOVE: In this timeline, Reese, not Sarah, is the naive one, and it's up to Sarah to bring him up to speed.

JOHN CONNOR

THE TERMINATOR FILMS HAVE ALWAYS HAD a messiah story lurking in the background. In the original film, Sarah is in danger because she will bear the savior of humankind (John Connor's initials are probably no accident), and she herself will be remembered as the mother of humanity. But there's a dark side to being the messiah that's only hinted at in the first movie.

Lussier says, "John is such a tragic force. Somebody who is cursed with so much pre-knowledge. Cursed with 'I will protect my father until I can send him to die for my creation.' He knows the weight of what he does, knowing that everything is about this moment. 'Everything must lead to here. I must get to this in order for us to have this victory.'"

The story for *Terminator Genisys* would take that underlying darkness in John's character and give it a shocking twist. When Skynet chooses a target for its nanocytes—someone to become the T-3000, a dark union of man and machine—it chooses the person who embodies not just resistance to technology run amok, but humanity's triumph over it.

John Connor.

"The technology has merged with him and overwritten him," explains Lussier. John doesn't choose to join the machines; once taken, he has no free will and is controlled by Skynet. But the John Connor T-3000 has his memories, his skills, his personality, his cunning, his strategic vision. He is John Connor turned against mankind—a very formidable adversary. And he is enhanced with what amounts to superpowers. He is physically stronger and more capable than any previous terminator. He is more than a match for Guardian. And over the planned trilogy, the writers intend for John Connor's story to be about the blurry line between human and machine intelligence, represented by the near future's version of Moses.

LEFT: Jason Clarke explores some of the darker corners of John Connor's psychology, including his manipulative side—John sends his own father back in time to die to ensure he will be conceived, after all. ABOVE: Father and son fighting side-by-side in the future war.

Once Sarah and Reese realize their attraction will bear such terrible fruit, the revelation complicates their love story. They know they should not conceive John, and as a practical matter, they can't—at least not as they did in the original movie. "John Connor in this timeline will never exist as their child the way he did," says Kalogridis. "Because that is a moment in time and that moment has passed. He can't be conceived exactly the same."

Director Alan Taylor says that while John Connor spends much of *Terminator Genisys* as the villain, "I think he was pretty nefarious even before he was a villain," pointing to his conscious decision to send his father back to die so that he can be born. "That set of relationships is really fraught and complicated. It's not simple heroism. Everyone is fighting the good fight, but there's a weird family dynamic going on there."

"When it came time to cast John Connor, there was only one name that everyone was talking about, which was Jason Clarke," says David Ellison. Ellison had befriended Clarke when the actor appeared in *Zero Dark Thirty*, which Megan Ellison's company had produced. Kalogridis had worked with him on *White House Down*, and he was her first choice as well. "There is a mesmerizing quality to him," she says. "The way that he, as an actor, can turn on a dime between being charming and scary. For me, he was perfect."

BELOW: John, once colonized by Skynet's nanocyte tech, becomes the T-3000. OPPOSITE TOP: Concept art shows the T-3000 coming unstuck when it comes into contact with a powerful magnetic field. OPPOSITE BOTTOM: The T-3000 retains John's memories, skills, and cunning but puts them in service of the machines.

Melissa Stubbs helped develop a fighting style for the John Connor T-3000. Several ideas were floated. Some wanted John to fight like a martial artist, but Stubbs argued that John, like Reese, would fight like a soldier. "I always go back to the Israeli martial art, Krav Maga, because it works, and it's practical. So we went with that."

Over the 2013 holidays, Clarke was on the phone almost daily with the filmmakers, kicking around ideas for the character. "We would tweak the script based on the conversations we had had with him," says Lussier, "because he came at it with such a grounded intelligence and a gut feeling of what the character was. None of it was surface; it was all really deep."

Jason Clarke proved to be quite a renaissance man: a rising movie star, a competitive driver who races his own Porsches, and an expert on men's clothing. Susan Matheson made a whirlwind trip to London to shop for costumes with Clarke and discovered that he had an encyclopedic knowledge of apparel. "I said, 'I have to hire you on my movies as a consultant,'" she recalls. "It was extraordinary."

Courtney found Clarke a generous scene partner who would work hard to support the other actors even when the camera wasn't on him. "He understands it's a team effort, and you've got to kind of bring it for your other actors so they can get where they need to go," says Courtney.

O'BRIEN

O'BRIEN IS A ROOKIE LAPD COP whose life is saved by Kyle Reese when they are attacked by the T-1000. He then spends thirty-three years working the mysterious case only to cross paths with Reese and Sarah when they travel to 2017 and becomes convinced of the truth of their time-travel story.

Veteran character actor J. K. Simmons, who plays the older O'Brien, says: "[In his later years] he is an SFPD inspector, a bit of a joke in the department, a bit of a sad sack, and a bit of a drinker, all due to his earlier encounter with our friends from the future."

Crucially, he is the one major character with no knowledge of the larger story of the war with the machines, Judgment Day, terminators, and time travel. As an innocent sizing up these people and events, he has to make choices about what to believe—and what to do about it.

David Ellison explains, "O'Brien is completely Patrick Lussier's brainchild. He wrote that entire character. When we finished the very first draft of the script, we sent it around to our office, and everybody came back: 'We love Sarah, we love Guardian, we love Kyle, we love John, but this new character O'Brian is fantastic. Every single second he's on-screen is gold.'"

ABOVE: As O'Brien, J. K. Simmons plays the one major character with no foreknowledge of the future. His decisions prove crucial.
OPPOSITE: Byung-hun Lee was determined to make his own take on the T-1000 as frightening as Robert Patrick's original.

T-1000

THE LIQUID METAL T-1000 in *Terminator 2* is a great movie villain, and that's not just a matter of visual effects. Actor Robert Patrick also helped create an eerily frightening character that quickly became a part of popular culture. Patrick was far less physically imposing than Schwarzenegger, but his terminator was arguably even more malevolent in its own way.

The task of portraying the soulless T-1000 in *Terminator Genisys* went to Korean star Byung-hun Lee. Lee says that because the T-1000 made such a lasting impression in *T2*, he felt a strong responsibility to the fans. "I stayed true to the original character while adding a few new moves of my own," he says. "In *Terminator Genisys,* we pushed the boundaries of what T-1000 can do with its liquid metal, and I'm so excited to see how the fans respond to it."

Once he got the role, Lee took himself back to what it was like to watch *T2* as a twelve-year-old, and he remembered how frightening the T-1000 was. When he discussed his approach to the T-1000 with Alan Taylor, Lee recalls he told the director that, "Overall T-1000 has to make people afraid—that is the most important thing we could not lose. Alan agreed, and we took it from there." Ultimately, Lee trained not by working on combat skills but by working on moving like a robot. "When I was a kid, I used to breakdance and pop-and-lock. It was so fun for me to put all that experience to good use on a film set."

05
THE DESIGNERS

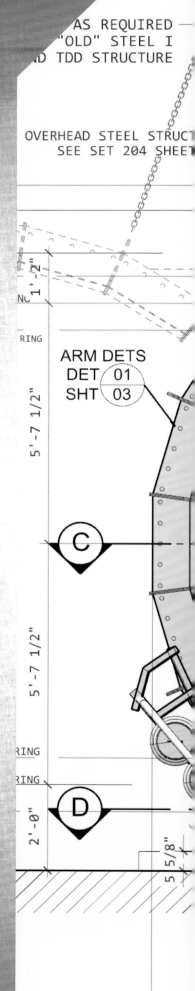

DIRECTOR ALAN TAYLOR HAD BEEN HIRED after a lengthy search for the right filmmaker to helm *Terminator Genisys*. At the time, Taylor, one of the directors of HBO's hit fantasy series *Game of Thrones*, was finishing work on *Marvel's Thor: The Dark World*, his first major film.

Taylor met with David Ellison and Goldberg and immediately impressed them with his focus on the character dynamics of the script.

"One of the first things that he talked about was the love story," says Ellison, "that the theme of this movie is a dysfunctional family that has to work perfectly in unison in order to beat the villain. He wasn't the guy who came in and just talked about, 'Here's how I'm going to shoot.'" After the meeting, Ellison persuaded Marvel chief Kevin Feige to let him have a sneak peek at *Thor: The Dark World* and was impressed. Somewhat to Taylor's own surprise, they offered him the job. "It's an intimidating thing to be on to the coattails of the James Cameron franchise," says Taylor. "But I saw that what they brought to it was delving into those relationships between Kyle and Sarah and the two strange father figures in John Connor and Guardian. That got me excited about trying to be part of it and made me think maybe I could contribute something."

> **"WHEN YOU PRESENT THE IMAGES, IT ISN'T NECESSARILY WHETHER THE IMAGES ARE RIGHT OR WRONG. IT'S MORE ABOUT THE REACTION THAT YOU GET FROM THE DIRECTOR AND THE DIALOGUE—WHETHER YOU'RE ACTUALLY COMMUNICATING."**

In the summer of 2013, with shooting starting in less than a year, Alan Taylor started the herculean task of putting together his crew for *Terminator Genisys*. Designers had to be hired, actors cast, sets and costumes constructed, locations and stages secured—a massive feat requiring the cooperation of a number of large departments.

Taylor's first hire was director of photography Kramer Morgenthau, who he had worked with in his television career and on *Thor: The Dark World*. "It is really important for me to have a very tight bond with the DP," says Taylor. "I knew it would be an adventure I wanted to share with somebody who would have a sure hand."

OPPOSITE: Plans show the impressive scale and detail of Neil Spisak's design for Guardian's homemade Time Displacement Device.

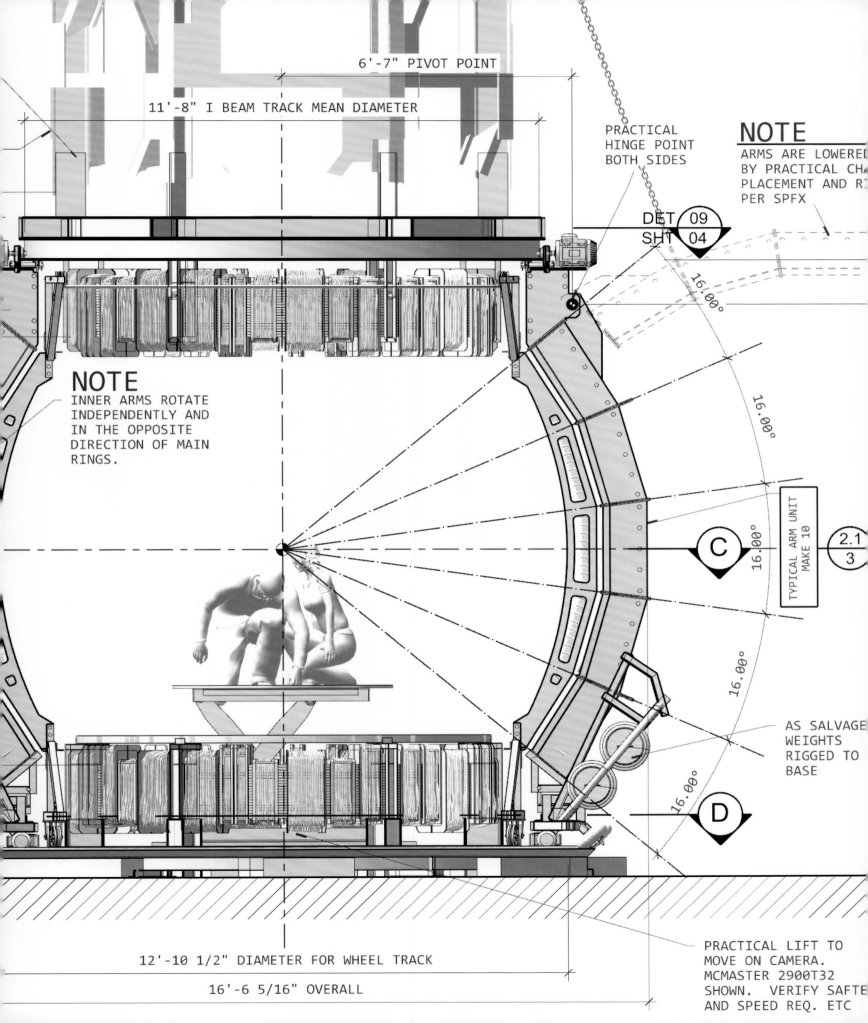

6'-7" PIVOT POINT

11'-8" I BEAM TRACK MEAN DIAMETER

PRACTICAL
HINGE POINT
BOTH SIDES

NOTE
ARMS ARE LOWERED
BY PRACTICAL CH/
PLACEMENT AND R1
PER SPFX

DET 09
SHT 04

16.00°

NOTE
INNER ARMS ROTATE
INDEPENDENTLY AND
IN THE OPPOSITE
DIRECTION OF MAIN
RINGS.

16.00°

TYPICAL ARM UNIT
MAKE 10

C

2.1
3

16.00°

16.00°

AS SALVAGE
WEIGHTS
RIGGED TO
BASE

16.00°

D

12'-10 1/2" DIAMETER FOR WHEEL TRACK

16'-6 5/16" OVERALL

PRACTICAL LIFT TO
MOVE ON CAMERA.
MCMASTER 2900T32
SHOWN. VERIFY SAFTE
AND SPEED REQ. ETC

Morgenthau felt there was a way to make visual references to *The Terminator* and *Terminator 2: Judgment Day* while giving *Terminator Genisys* a more contemporary feel. "The original film has very much a film noir look," says Morgenthau. "*T2* is a little edgier. And they created this machine universe that's very cool and very brightly lit."

Much of the team that joined the project came from Skydance or from Paramount and had never worked with Taylor. On Paramount's suggestion, Taylor hired production designer Neil Spisak, whose long list of credits included Sam Raimi's *Spider-Man* trilogy and, most recently, *Teenage Mutant Ninja Turtles* for Paramount.

For production designers like Spisak, the first job interview with the director and producers provides a rare creative opportunity. Lacking prior instruction, they have a free hand to create and present images for the film as they envision it. "When you present the images, it isn't necessarily whether the images are right or wrong," says Spisak. "It's more about the reaction that you get from

the director and the dialogue—whether you're actually communicating." If that communication is good, the designer might be hired, even if the ideas and images from the first interview don't end up in the film's final design.

Taylor made a connection with Spisak, the director recalls. "It was fun to brainstorm with him," says Taylor. "He was very energetic and kept surprising us with sets and giving us more than we asked for." As it happened, one of Spisak's ideas surprised Taylor and Ellison: What if the 2029 "work camp" seen in the battle early in the film was set in the ruins of LAX airport? This compelling notion helped him land the post of production designer and was incorporated into the film.

Coming to the project via a Skydance connection was costume designer Susan Matheson. Matheson had impressed Ellison and Goldberg with her designs for *Jack Reacher,* Skydance's Tom Cruise action picture. "She'd spent hours in bars in Pittsburgh doing research, drawing sketches of what people look like and what they

TOP AND OPPOSITE: Production designer Neil Spisak pitched the idea that the machines had turned LAX airport into a work camp. The idea became an anchor of the Future War imagery.

57

ABOVE AND OPPOSITE TOP:
Costume designer Susan Matheson
conceived improvised armor made
from scavenged materials for the
resistance fighters. OPPOSITE
BOTTOM: John Connor and his elite
team wearing Matheson's battle
armor.

were wearing," says Ellison. "We were blown away by that level of commitment to research and accuracy, while still making beautiful wardrobe."

What they did not know when they asked her to meet about *Terminator Genisys* was that she'd been dreaming of this call her entire career. Matheson had gone to Vassar College in New York aiming to become an actress but, at age eighteen, saw *The Terminator*, and that, along with *The Road Warrior*, inspired her to switch to costume design. She even designed a production of *Macbeth* at school, where she dressed Macbeth in a leather jacket inspired by the one worn by Schwarzenegger in *The Terminator*. After years studying sculpture in Japan and designing Barbie outfits at Mattel, she turned to films, and by 2013, she had a long resume of hits. Yet though she was obsessed with science fiction, she'd never designed for the genre. Then came the call to interview for *Terminator Genisys*.

"I thought it was some kind of practical joke," she recalls. "Is this real? Because this is what I wanted for so long." She came in for her *Terminator Genisys* interview not expecting to get the job, but Taylor was won over by "her insane level of enthusiasm," as he puts it. "It's certainly infectious and irresistible." When the call came that the job was hers, she recounts, "I actually started shrieking. I don't think I've ever been more excited to get a film."

Some others who came onto the project had deep connections to the franchise itself. John Rosengrant of Legacy Effects came on board to work with prosthetic makeup. Rosengrant had worked on every Terminator film, starting out under the late, great creature-maker and puppeteer Stan Winston. Rosengrant was especially interested in the idea of Schwarzenegger as an older cyborg. "I love the idea that they are embracing who he is in a very logical way and have an explanation for it, storywise."

REBEL BATTLE ARMOR:

- PROVIDES VITAL ORGAN PROTECTION
  AGAINST PLASMA HIT USING CAPTURED
  PLASMA-RESISTANT MATERIAL
- MODULAR CONFIGURATION AND
  RETROFIT READY
- MOUNT FOR SMOKE CANNISTER ON BACK

06

THE THREE LOOKS

ONE CRUCIAL DECISION in the early stages of the production of *Terminator Genisys* was how many of the scenes would require physical sets and how much of the shoot could be accomplished with green screens and digital effects. Those decisions would ripple outward to the construction crew; the physical special effects supervisor, who must plan for pyrotechnics; and the stunt coordinators.

Spisak and visual effects supervisor Janek Sirrs shared the philosophy that it's always better to get something "in camera"—that is, to shoot it for real—than to "fix it in post," but some settings were simply too huge to build. Constructing the LAX-sized futuristic work camp, for example, would simply be too expensive, so the task would fall to the VFX team.

Matheson, too, was feeling the pressure. "The only way that you can handle a movie of this size without feeling overwhelmed," she says, "is to break it down into small pieces. And you take it piece by piece. You deal with each little piece at a time until the end of the movie completes the puzzle."

> **"THE ONLY WAY THAT YOU CAN HANDLE A MOVIE OF THIS SIZE WITHOUT FEELING OVERWHELMED IS TO BREAK IT DOWN INTO SMALL PIECES. AND YOU TAKE IT PIECE BY PIECE."**

Spisak and the designers conceived three distinct looks for the film: one for the 2029 "Future War" that opens the film, one for the 1984 sequences that recall the original film, and one for the 2017 sequences from the latter section of the story. Spisak says, "Jumping between the three time periods had, for me, always been a little bit of a complication in terms of keeping it straight and understanding where you are. It was important to me to differentiate those three realities."

OPPOSITE: The center of the Time Displacement Device was built as a practical set in New Orleans. Here it is seen as a final frame from *Terminator Genisys*.

1984

Spisak began with the 1984 sequences, which pay homage to *The Terminator*. "We were trying to get as close in feel as possible," he says, "and yet reinvent it for the new version of Terminator." He calls the overall feel for 1984 "an incandescent, golden-glow world, taking our cue from 1984 downtown Los Angeles."

The Griffith Observatory scene in *Terminator Genisys* starts as a precise shot-for-shot recreation of the scene from *The Terminator*—until the stories radically diverge, that is. Morgenthau deliberately changed the lighting slightly, going for a more magenta tone than the original's blue.

"Adam Greenberg, the original DP of *The Terminator*, did beautiful work with hard light," says Morgenthau. "That still really holds up, and we experimented with some of that noir-ish type lightning." Prop master Diana Burton found the same model of coin-operated telescope seen in the original shots and made some rubber replicas so that, when Guardian faces off with the younger T-800, they are able to use the telescopes as weapons.

Matheson begins her design process with the psychology of the characters and likes to kick that around with the actors. "Then I say, 'Well, how will it

translate into clothing?' Because if you just go out and
start shopping, you end up with a fiasco on your hands."
Her first conversation after meeting with Taylor was
with Schwarzenegger. They discussed Guardian's years
among people, raising Sarah, trying to blend in and avoid
suspicion, but unable to do some of the things a human
would do. Guardian's outfit would feature some of the
elements of the original *The Terminator* and *T2* costumes
but with adjustments for his character. For his dramatic
entrance at the observatory scene, he wears cargo pants,
tactical boots, and a leather jacket. The jacket is in a classic

terminator style, but since he's a good guy, he gets a
hoodie underneath to soften his look. Guardian can also
be seen briefly in the original leather Harley jacket from
The Terminator in the 1973 flashback scene.

One dilemma for Matheson was how to make
Schwarzenegger a match for his younger doppelganger.
A terminator wouldn't lose bulk with age, and though
Schwarzenegger was still in great shape, he didn't have
the same physique as thirty years earlier. Taylor suggested
building a muscle suit for him to wear under his costume,
and Matheson raised the idea with Schwarzenegger.

ABOVE: Concept art shows the
moment where Kyle Reese's story
swerves into unknown territory
when Sarah and Guardian interrupt
his encounter with the T-1000 by
crashing an armored truck into
the fray.

"He said, 'No, no, no. That will not be necessary,'" says Matheson. A month later, he arrived in a skintight workout shirt. "He'd completely transformed himself," she recalls. "I said, 'Have you been working out?' And he looks at me and says, 'No, not at all.' And of course I knew he was playing with me. He had pretty much brought himself back to the same waist and same shoulder measurements as 1984. I think the idea that I would need to build a muscle suit for Arnold Schwarzenegger was beyond comprehension, and he was damn sure that he was going to fix it."

Recreating the 1984 costumes proved fiendishly difficult for Matheson. Some of the original off-the-rack items were common then but are now rare. Matheson's prep became a treasure hunt. Kyle Reese's costume had to be a perfect match, head to toe, for what Michael Biehn wore in the original movie, but his military trench coat was unlike those in surplus stores in 2013. "It was a lighter fabric, and it had a little bit more of a drape to it," says Matheson. "Because it was the 80s, it had more of a dropped shoulder. A lot of punk rockers used to wear it with highly laced up Doc Martens and skinny jeans." Matheson tried building replicas of the coat with various fabrics but was growing concerned. "It was like Goldilocks and the Three Bears—too hot, too cold, too lumpy. It just wasn't feeling like the original trench coat." Then her crew went shopping and found a vintage coat in a thrift store. She put it on Jai Courtney, who was to play Reese, and had a "Eureka!" moment; it was *the* trench coat. She hunted around on the web and found about a dozen of them. One problem solved.

Reese's Nike Vandal sneakers were also problematic. *The Terminator* features a close-up shot of Reese pulling the

Vandals' velcro shut, so fans knew *exactly* what those shoes look like. Matheson's online research revealed that fans were even blogging about their hunt for this exact model, so it was clear no substitute would do. Having convinced Adidas to make vegan basketball shoes for Woody Harrelson in *Semi-Pro*, she thought she could convince Nike to recreate its vintage Vandal design.

At first, Nike demurred and suggested she use their build-your-own-shoe site to make something close, using their Air Force One shoe as a base.

"I'm a sneaker nerd," says Matheson, "and the Air Force One base is nothing like the Nike Vandal." She asked Paramount to intercede with Nike, lest fans call them out for cheating on the sneakers: "I said, 'This is something we will get eaten alive for. Not only will we look bad but Nike will look bad.'" Finally, Nike agreed to stop a production line and retool it to create a special batch of Vandals for the film. The shoes would prove to be among the most coveted items on the set, at least by one measure: About a dozen went missing during off-hours.

While Matheson largely enjoyed success in her hunt for '80s fashion artifacts, some items couldn't be found and had to be re-created by hand; for example, the military coat worn by one of the observatory punks and appropriated by the T-800. ("Your clothes. Give them to me.") The single most challenging item proved to be the graffiti-strewn T-shirt Schwarzenegger wore under his leather jacket in *The Terminator*. The original was a surf T-shirt that had been bought on L.A.'s trendy Melrose Avenue, and the replica had to be hand-painted using blown-up stills of the film as reference.

ABOVE: Susan Matheson persuaded Nike to do a production run of the long-retired Vandal sneakers Reese wore in *The Terminator*. Here, Jai Courtney hurriedly grabs them from a shelf. OPPOSITE LEFT: It took a lucky find in a thrift shop and some adept web searches to match Reese's original trench coat. OPPOSITE RIGHT: Concept art shows the attention to detail Susan Matheson brought to replicating Kyle's costume from the original movie.

Sarah Connor's look would be neither the soft waitress of *The Terminator* nor the steely warrior of *T2*, but something in between—with a distinctly '80s vibe. "I started to think about the seminal pieces that all women in 1984 were wearing," says Matheson. "A lot of women wore Doc Martens with dresses at that time. A lot of people wore motorcycle jackets with dresses and with jeans. So I thought, by putting her in a motorcycle jacket, we'd almost echo what Arnold had worn in the original film in 1984. I wanted to put her in something that did connect us with the original film." Her 1984 outfit is Doc Martens, cargo pants, and a motorcycle jacket; Sarah's apple hasn't fallen far from Guardian's tree.

Re-creating the weapons of 1984 was mostly a matter of research and legwork. Prop master Diana Burton found the same model pistol the terminator used in *The Terminator* and matched other guns from the film. (She also found weapons from *T2*, including a Browning, a Desert Eagle pistol, and even a Minigun.) One new prop for the story would be a firearm that could kill a T-800. That was a

thorny plot issue, since it took the entire length of the first movie to kill the original T-800, and no gun seemed to work against it. But Burton turned up a weapon that existed in 1984 and just might have the punch for the job: a Barrett sniper rifle that could fire depleted uranium rounds. The writers consulted with James Cameron, who signed off on the idea that it could take down a T-800. "The weapon was actually available in 1984, just barely," says Taylor. "It wasn't available commercially, but resourceful people like Sarah Connor and the Guardian could have gotten a hold of it."

2029

The 2029 Future War sequence that opens *Terminator Genisys* gets a distinctly different look from 1984. Morgenthau would shoot it in a desaturated cyan tone, and much of the vast battlefield and the machines that patrol it would have to be added with visual effects. Since the specifics of the action sequences weren't yet planned, the Future War sets would have to be flexible, capable of being reconfigured, and used in multiple ways. "It was about creating a playground for stunts, for second unit, for first unit, for visual effects to be able to work with," says Spisak.

Creating a post-apocalyptic look that hadn't been seen before was a challenge for all concerned. "There's a lot of competition in that world in terms of past movies," says Spisak. In *Terminator Genisys*'s Future War, the shiny, metallic hardness of the machines contrasts with the patched-together look of the human militia. The post–Judgment Day future has always looked rough in the Terminator franchise, but the *Terminator Genisys* designers added a more specific sense of place. Resistance fighters and captives alike have been scavenging the ruins of Los Angeles, so their costumes contain items from

ABOVE: Concept art shows a firefight pitting the resistance against Hunter-Killers and Spider Tanks. OPPOSITE BOTTOM: The T-800 endoskeletons in *Terminator Genisys* are subtly different from the original and just as terrifying.

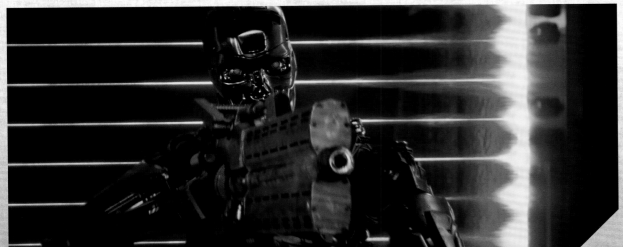

L.A.'s many ethnic enclaves and include such ubiquitous SoCal items as Lakers and Dodgers t-shirts.

The resistance has repurposed corporate vehicles into war machines, made shoulder pads out of old tires, and fashioned body armor out of anything from paintball gear to license plates and street signs. "Quite a few pieces we added to the armor were actually made from cutting up rugged rubber car mats," says Matheson. The elite fighters, like John Connor and Kyle Reese, get the best gear the humans can muster, while the rest make do with what they can.

Creating that post-apocalyptic look was a particular thrill for science fiction buff Matheson. She'd studied sculpture in Japan, and that proved useful for crafting found objects into costumes. Her own team of thirty built costumes for 300 principals and extras for the Future War alone. Then those costumes went into small cement mixers to be tumbled with pumice stones. In went car-mat armor, motocross and paintball pads, kneepads, and clothing. Says Matheson: "These cement mixers were going all day, every day for months."

There was also a team of "ager-dyers," headed by Gildardo Tobon, a veteran of the aging work that went into the costumes on the first two *Pirates of the Caribbean* films. "He has an incredible sensibility for making things feel old and used and thrashed, but real," says Matheson. The ager-dyers glued sand to clothes, over-dyed them, and sprayed

them with photo-sensitive chemicals. Matheson says, "I would show things to the director and the producers, and they would be very suspect, like, 'How is this ever going to work?' and then by the time Gil and his team were done with the stuff, the pieces were unrecognizable."

Futuristic weapon design was Burton's task. Some resistance fighters have regular guns scavenged and cobbled together, but regular projectile weapons are nearly useless against the machines. "The idea behind most of the (future) weapons was that they were plasma technology, which was effective against terminators," explains Burton. "The rebels gained access to some of the technology developed by the terminators and then used that technology against them."

She drew up several weapon designs. Besides the plasma rifles carried by resistance fighters, John Connor uses an intimidating 50-caliber, vehicle-mounted plasma cannon. There's also a more primitive plasma rifle seen in a flashback to John Connor's first meeting with Kyle Reese.

Many Future War weapons are modified AK-47 rifles fitted with specially built "plasma rifle" outer casings to disguise them. "It was really important to us to have the plasma rifles be realistic," explains Ellison. "The traditional way is to make a plastic gun and fake the recoil. We thought that was going to look phony. So we modified actual working guns. We wanted to make it feel as real and authentic as possible."

ABOVE: In many instances, prop master Diana Burton created futuristic-looking weapons by modifying modern-day guns. OPPOSITE TOP: John Connor's truck-mounted plasma cannon is a fearsome weapon. OPPOSITE BOTTOM: The plasma weapons wielded by the T-800 endos were rendered using digital effects.

Since there are real rifles inside the shell, those guns could be fired on camera. That made for real muzzle flashes and gave the actors and stunt men an authentic recoil. Real firearms get hot, though, so there had to be three versions of each "plasma rifle" shell: guns that were set for automatic firing (and so would get very hot) got an all-metal casing; guns that were set for semi-automatic (and so did not get as hot) got a part-metal, part-rubber casing; and for guns that would be in on-screen explosions or used in stunts, there was an all-rubber, non-firing version.

Of course there are plenty of plasma weapons in the hands of the machines, too, especially the gleaming T-800 endoskeletons that guard the work camp and battle the resistance. "They have the big plasma canons that I had to create as well," says Burton. "It was a completely one-off design. Those were completely metal, and I put lights and stuff in them."

Once the weapons designs were approved, it took six weeks for them to be fabricated by a model shop. Burton's plasma weapons are a prominent feature of the Future War, but the physical versions of the plasma cannons she built for the "Endos," the skinless, fleshless T-800 robots that patrol this scorched earth, will not actually be seen on-screen. Since there are no real T-800 terminators to walk around the set, stand-ins were hired to take their place. The stand-ins were digitally replaced with CG Endos in postproduction, so the Endos' plasma cannons became CG as well.

In designing the plasma cannon, Burton inadvertently came to embody one of *Terminator Genisys*'s central themes: the union of human and machine. For to design a weapon like a machine, you have to get into their mechanical mindset. "You have to think that machines are creating them, so they're not thinking about bells and whistles or flair or anything," she says. "They're thinking completely utilitarian. If you're thinking like a machine, you're not going to make a really cool-looking weapon that a human would have designed."

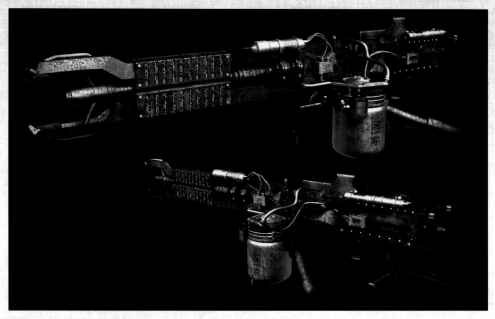

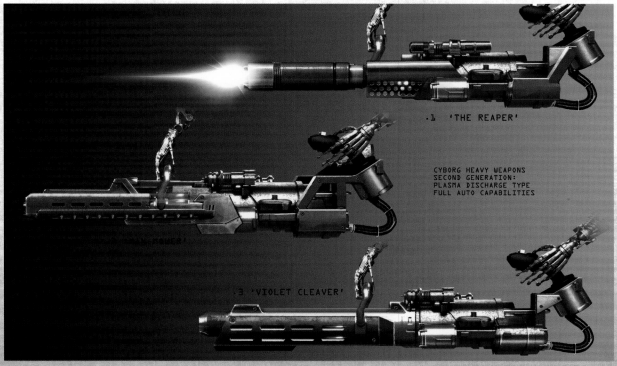

.1 'THE REAPER'

CYBORG HEAVY WEAPONS
SECOND GENERATION:
PLASMA DISCHARGE TYPE
FULL AUTO CAPABILITIES

.3 'VIOLET CLEAVER'

2017

"When we got to 2017," says David Ellison, "we wanted everything to feel unbelievably slick and beautiful and full of life, so every time you looked around at our world, you understood what our heroes were fundamentally fighting to save." And since 2017 is so close to the film's release date, Spisak decided it would get a more naturalistic treatment than either 2029 or 1984. "It has a crisper, stronger, sharper kind of light, more of an LED kind of feel," he says. By the time Reese and Sarah jump through time from 1984 to 2017, they know they are headed for the ultimate showdown with Skynet. So when they acquire clothes, Sarah gets a tactical

vest and other combat clothing. Practicality and survival are the only things on her mind. Guardian, on the other hand, doesn't go through the TDD; he waits out the years from 1984 to 2017 preparing for that showdown, buying weapons with money earned working construction. By the time Reese and Sarah show up, he looks very much like a construction worker. "Who knew the terminator would ever wear jeans and construction worker boots?" says Matheson.

The designers' embrace of the picture's three looks exemplified Spisak's favorite thing about working on *Terminator Genisys*. "As the production designer, I suppose

ABOVE: Concept art shows Guardian's fight with the T-3000 in Cyberdyne's headquarters. LEFT: Cyberdyne's San Francisco HQ is based on Oracle's corporate offices in Redwood City.

RIGHT: Concept art shows the moment where Sarah and Reese's plans go awry when they materialize in 2017 in the middle of a busy freeway. BELOW: Storyboards of the arrival scene show the stunt work needed when Reese is hit by a car, breaking its windshield. BOTTOM RIGHT: Concept art details the iconic bubble of energy that accompanies time travel in the Terminator franchise.

everybody thinks you design everything, but you take everybody's contribution and mold it into one cohesive thing," says Spisak. "All of the art directors, the decorator, the prop master, the director, and producers all sort of got into the spirit of where I was going with it. It doesn't always happen, but on this, they all were able to contribute, so it got very rich and complicated, and it helped make the movie more coherent."

07 TRAINING THE CAST

IN NOVEMBER 2013, the start of filming on *Terminator Genisys* was just five months off, but there was still a huge amount of preparation to be done. While sets and costumes were constructed, the actors built themselves up for their roles.

Jai Courtney, a veteran of action films, was plenty fit and adept with weapons and stage fighting but decided to drop twenty pounds before shooting began. "If you think about a soldier in a resistance army in the future, these are guys that probably don't get fed three times a day," he explains. "I spent hours and hours walking uphill on a treadmill, pretty much eating salmon constantly, and drinking more water than I thought possible."

> "IF YOU THINK ABOUT A SOLDIER IN A RESISTANCE ARMY IN THE FUTURE, THESE ARE GUYS THAT PROBABLY DON'T GET FED THREE TIMES A DAY. I SPENT HOURS AND HOURS WALKING UPHILL ON A TREADMILL, PRETTY MUCH EATING SALMON CONSTANTLY, AND DRINKING MORE WATER THAN I THOUGHT POSSIBLE."

Emilia Clarke faced an especially grueling few months; she needed to pack on some muscle and become convincing on-screen as a trained fighter. That meant a regimen of weight, fight, and firearms training, driving lessons, and, on top of that, dialect coaching, since the British-born actress would have to sound as Californian as Linda Hamilton's Sarah Connor. Veteran stuntwoman Melissa Stubbs, who had been hired to be Clarke's stunt double, was put in charge of turning Clarke into a fierce warrior. Stubbs, who has been a stunt performer since her teens, says that being picked on by her older brothers helped spur her lifelong interest in martial arts. "When a person is in shape and training hard, they walk into a room with confidence," she says. It's that kind of confidence that she would give to Clarke—along with more muscular arms and a lower body fat percentage. Clarke cut out carbs and trained fiercely. Her day would start with an hour of hard cardio before breakfast—often running on sand or on hills— with more cardio or weight training later in the day, as well as her various other classes and training sessions. "This poor kid didn't have a minute of sleep," says Stubbs. But after the

RIGHT: Emilia Clarke underwent rigorous weapons training for the role of Sarah Connor.

ABOVE: Emilia Clarke unleashes a shotgun blast during filming of the confrontation with the T-1000. OPPOSITE: Emilia Clarke was trained by Melissa Stubbs to become an adept hand-to-hand fighter.

initial shock to her system, Clarke thrived. She says, "Whilst all those elements were needed for the role, from an acting point of view, it was so wonderful to have that. Because it just throws you right into it. When you have all those skills at your fingertips, you feel more engrossed in the part, which is so good."

Armorer Harry Lu gave her weapons instruction. "Harry was the secret star of the show," says Clarke. "He gave me not only an understanding of how to handle the weapons, but we talked survival, we talked self-defense."

Clarke also turned out to have a wicked spinning right back-fist. "She could take someone's head off," says Stubbs. "I said, 'Do you have an older brother?' and she said, 'Yes.' I said, 'Honey, you've hit him before,' and she said, 'Why, yes, I have.'"

Clarke says that she loves kickboxing and fighting and didn't get her fill on *Terminator Genisys*. "I hope that I get to do more [in the sequels]. I spoke to Patrick and Laeta about it, and I'm pretty sure that's in the cards, which would be amazing."

08 POUND GROUND

WHILE FANS ARE OFTEN REMARKABLY SAVVY about film production, few are familiar with the art of crafting a shooting schedule. Alan Taylor admits he's glad it's handled by others. "Frequently, you start off with something that makes sense and is rational, and then it winds up being something absolutely loony based on an actor's schedule and availability, and weather, and what sets will be ready to go first." *Terminator Genisys* would shoot for eighty days, all but the last eight in New Orleans. First and second units would both be working from the start of shooting. First unit would mostly shoot the 1984 sequences with Schwarzenegger and company, while second unit would mostly shoot the Future War. The action scenes would need around eighty stunt performers and three stunt coordinators: John Stoneham Jr., Gary Hymes, and Melissa Stubbs. There would be multiple stunt units, so while one performed, another could prep for the next day's action.

Schwarzenegger came with two of his own stunt doubles, both of whom have been with him for years. One, Billy Lucas, serves as Schwarzenegger's fight double. "We called him the ground-pounding double," says Stoneham, using a stuntman's term for someone whose job is to take hard falls over and over again. "Arnold is sixty-seven, and you can't have him pounding the ground." The second double is for driving scenes. There were also second-unit doubles and stand-ins for Schwarzenegger as well.

> "YOU HAVE ARNOLD WALKING LIKE THE TERMINATOR UP AND DOWN THE HALLWAY, AND THE TWO STUNT DOUBLES ARE TRAILING BEHIND HIM, TRYING TO WALK LIKE ARNOLD."

One day in the production office, Susan Matheson overheard the stunt doubles quizzing Schwarzenegger about the correct terminator walk. "Finally he said, 'Follow me,'" she says. "You have Arnold walking like the terminator up and down the hallway, and the two stunt doubles are trailing behind him, trying to walk like Arnold." They didn't do so well at first, but soon the hallway was hosting a parade of three perfectly synced terminators.

Stubbs worked closely with the actors on fight choreography. "I really love the art of fighting," she says. "I love putting myself in the character's head. Trying to figure out how a character would approach this." Courtney proved adept at picking up action moves, though.

RIGHT: Jason Clarke and Arnold Schwarzenegger perform a fight scene in front of green screens. Note Schwarzenegger's impassive expression—as Schwarzenegger reminded the stunt team, terminators do not feel pain.

"We'd choreograph a fight sequence," says Stubbs, "and they would schedule two hours with us to teach him the choreography. He would have it right away. I'd be like, 'OK, you're done. Do you want to just do something fun?'"

Staging a fight for a cyborg, though, was a thorny problem. Normally, says Stubbs, fight choreography is cause-and-effect; one fighter hits, the other reacts. But terminators are essentially impervious to blows and don't react to them. The earlier Terminator films built that idea into their fight scenes. Schwarzenegger's terminator characters in *T2* and *Terminator 3: Rise of the Machines* would avoid extended hand-to-hand fighting with other terminators because it was a useless tactic;

no terminator was powerful enough to damage another with just a punch or kick. "In the past films, the terminators fought each other in a certain way," says Stubbs. "They smashed each other. They would drive each other through structures; throw each other; grab large, heavy objects; and smash the opponent with them. Or they would use firepower, large caliber weapons."

The T-3000 was to be different, though. Due to its nanotech construction and advanced materials, it was capable of injuring a T-800 like Guardian in a fight. So Stubbs built Guardian's reactions into the choreography of a battle between the aging robot and the T-3000. "The T-3000 can flow like sand," says Stubbs. "How is the

antiquated terminator going to fight with this nanocyte, ever-moving matter? It automatically repairs itself. But magnets are his kryptonite."

Stubbs admits being "a little intimidated" by Schwarzenegger at first. "He's from an entirely different generation of action movies," she says, "but he was so warm, and he was such a gentleman and so respectful. He moves well still. He looks great." By the time they were finished working together, Stubbs got to know Schwarzenegger well enough and was able to anticipate what he would approve or reject in his fight choreography.

09
BUILD IT UP

DIRECTOR OF PHOTOGRAPHY Kramer Morgenthau and production designer Neil Spisak faced an enormous task, both because of the scale of *Terminator Genisys* and the high expectations that come with any Terminator film.

Morgenthau conducted extensive tests with the actors to pin down just the right angles for shooting them. Tests included direct or softer lighting, lighting from different angles, different lenses, and different heights for the camera. He chose the Arri Alexa digital cinema camera for shooting, making *Terminator Genisys* the first film in the franchise to be captured digitally.

He also selected Panavision C-series anamorphic lenses, some of which date back to the 1960s and 70s. "They give the Alexa a softer, painterly look and take some of the electronic hardness off the picture," he says. The anamorphic lenses gave the images widescreen scale and an "epic look," says Morgenthau. "It's a great horizontal canvas that brings the best out of the big sets and big set pieces."

> "THE TIME DISPLACEMENT DEVICE SETS ENDED UP BEING SOME OF THE MOST IMPRESSIVE AND SOME OF THE MOST DEMANDING FOR THE CREW."

Terminator Genisys would indeed have some enormous sets—notably the Time Displacement Devices—and only a few months to build them. Production designer Neil Spisak credits his art directors and construction crew for somehow getting the work done under the gun. As many as 150 builders were at work on the show at its peak. Much of their work took place in huge hangers NASA had built in New Orleans for construction of the Space Shuttle; those buildings are now rented out to film shoots to become giant sound stages. Other sets were built inside a former home improvement store space.

The TDD sets ended up being some of the most impressive and some of the most demanding for the crew. Three TDDs are seen in the story, one in each of the major time periods. The 2029 TDD is seen first—the machine that sends the killer T-800 and Reese back to 1984. The set was large but only partially built and augmented with green screens so digitally created set extensions could fill out the enormous space. The 2017 TDD was also a large set, boasting a more industrial-looking and less futuristic design. It, too, was a partial set with green screens representing a much larger space.

RIGHT: Guardian's homemade Time Displacement Device, built underground, echoes the design of the 2029 version but is much more compact.

Taylor does not particularly like to shoot against green screens, he says, "[but] it was beyond us to build the sets to scale. At least the actors could be in that environment and interacting physically with it, so that helped."

The 1984 TDD is the only one of the three TDD sets to be built as a complete physical set. In the story, it has been built by Guardian out of scavenged parts and assembled in secret in tunnels beneath a power plant. It's "sort of a Frankenstein version of a machine," says Morgenthau. "The machine itself is a glowing monster that's creating light sort of magically but also by plasma surging through it."

In the TDDs, the time travelers climb onto a platform surrounded by huge spinning rings. Originally the spinning rings were to have been all CG, but there was a late decision to build them as sets, in part to give the actors something tangible to act with. A crew of eight effects technicians worked for two months solid to prepare them for shooting. "It's a beautiful piece," says special effects supervisor Mark Hawker. "I don't think anybody will ever realize the amount of work that went into the movement."

If the intention of the set was to help the actors, it worked. Jai Courtney expected to only be playing against green screen and was impressed at how much was built for real. "All that makes it a lot easier," says Courtney. "The less you have to fake it, the more you're investing and believing the world you're in."

Another formidable set built for *Terminator Genisys* is the tunnel area where Sarah faces off against the shape-shifting T-1000. Taylor came up with the idea of making the tunnel a roundhouse-like hub, so danger could come from any direction. But Sarah and Guardian have rigged the tunnel with acid, turning it into a deathtrap for the T-1000. "Neil did a brilliant job of realizing it," says Taylor. "The effects rig was incredibly complicated. We had real tanks up there with real liquid that had to spray on cue and drench Byung-hun Lee [the actor playing the T-1000]. So it was a waterproof set with all kinds of technical issues."

The set for Guardian's ample armory proved to be an opportunity to add Easter eggs for fans. It's stocked with

OPPOSITE: A staggering amount of detail went into the 1984 Time Displacement Device set. BELOW: A vast network of tunnels was built on set in New Orleans for the scene where Sarah, Kyle, and Guardian, lure the T-1000 into a trap.

ABOVE: Concept art shows Cyberdyne's Time Displacement device in 2017. RIGHT: Various concept designs for the central element of the Time Displacement Device.

around 500 guns, 80 percent of them real and the rest specially constructed props. Armorer Harry Lu incorporated guns from other films, especially the earlier Terminator films; look for the 7-inch long slide .45 pistol and the AR-18 rifle from *The Terminator* and the M79 (a grenade launcher) and M134 Minigun from *T2*. Some lethal new weapons were introduced to the saga, too—Clarke says learning to use the powerful MK19 grenade launcher was the toughest part of her training. "Holding a 50-pound gun and firing it repetitively is hard," she says, laughing at the memory. "That was literally a couple of gun sessions just managing to hold it with one hand. The weight of these guns is so huge, and the kickback is so strong—you really have to have everything in the right place posture-wise."

"Doing that stuff is wicked fun," she adds.

Armorer Harry Lu became one of the most popular people on the set, yet he is bit of a mystery man. He will admit to having been a civil engineer who changed careers and wound up doing some kind of work—he declines to say exactly what—that caused him to become a firearms expert. He found his way to movie work and became a top film armorer. His resume stretches back to *T2*.

Lu's duties on a film include safety, choosing physical modifications for the guns, mixing powder to get the proper smoke and muzzle flash, and compliance with local gun laws. Law enforcement and the military prefer as little muzzle flash as possible, so Lu adds chemicals to commercial gunpowder to change the color (due to toxic fumes, the heavy metals used in fireworks are off limits) and adjusts each gun's blanking device to create a starburst, cone, or omnidirectional flash. He also oversees security for the guns. The armory was guarded around the clock, and any guns used by the principals were kept in a vault.

For one 1984 alley scene that was shot adjacent to a New Orleans hotel, noise restrictions meant the production couldn't fire an actual gun at all. He solved the problem with a "non-gun" that resembles a real revolver but uses an electronic squib instead of a powder charge. Satisfied that their guests wouldn't be frightened, hotel management approved the solution just days before the scene was to be shot.

On all the productions he works on, Lu also does a last, subtle safety check as he hands the actors their guns on the set. "If the person you're giving it to is not—how should I say it—'all there,' he or she could cause great bodily harm," says Lu. So he keeps his hand over the trigger and looks into the eyes of each actor, making sure they look sober and sane. Happily, he reports, he never had to withhold a gun from an actor on *Terminator Genisys*.

OPPOSITE TOP: Concept art of Guardian's hidden armory. OPPOSITE BOTTOM Kyle Reese adapts quickly to the weaponry of 1984. ABOVE: Every terminator trap needs its own acid bath for eliminating downed machines once and for all.

10
BLOOD & SILICONE

THE TERMINATOR FILMS HAVE ALWAYS pushed the boundaries of prosthetic makeup, and *Terminator Genisys* would be no exception. Thousands of individual prosthetic appliances would be prepared for shooting, ranging from John Connor's facial scars to Guardian's wounds. On the original film, prosthetic makeup was handled by the legendary, multi–Oscar-winning Stan Winston. On *Terminator Genisys,* those duties fell to Legacy Effects, a company formed by staff members of the Stan Winston Studio when Winston passed away in 2008. Some sixty-five craftsmen at Legacy worked on *Terminator Genisys,* with three being present on the set as part of the makeup crew.

> "COUNTING THOSE THAT WOULD GO ON SCHWARZENEGGER AND EACH OF HIS DOUBLES, LEGACY CREATED THOUSANDS OF APPLIANCES FOR GUARDIAN ALONE. "

John Rosengrant, who led Legacy's team on *Terminator Genisys,* had worked on every previous Terminator film and has seen technology for prosthetic makeup change radically since Winston created the original terminator's wounds. "The materials have gotten more realistic looking," explains Rosengrant. "Now we're dealing with more silicones and prosthetic transfers. They can be applied very quickly, they blend in speedier, they have a translucence and depth to them, and they move better." Counting those that would go on Schwarzenegger and each of his doubles, Legacy created thousands of appliances for Guardian alone.

Nowadays silicone appliances are often complemented by digital visual effects. A makeup artist can put an appliance onto an actor to simulate a wound, then paint what's inside that wound pale green. That green screen hue is then replaced in visual effects production with whatever is supposed to be revealed in the wound, such as Guardian's endoskeleton.

One of Legacy's simplest but most effective creations was a Schwarzenegger mask for the stunt men and doubles, fixed in Schwarzenegger's grim "terminator" expression. Goldberg says the mask looked "scarily" like Schwarzenegger. After Billy Lucas wore it to shoot a stunt, Schwarzenegger happened by when Goldberg and others were watching playback of the shot. "He goes, 'When did I do that?'" says Goldberg. "We said, 'That's not you. That's Billy.' He looked at it, and he's, like, 'Really? Well, what the hell do you need me for?'"

OPPOSITE: Created by the team at Legacy Effects, these prosthetic T-800 legs (modeled on molds of Schwarzenegger's early '80s physique) are used in the scene where the terminator is brought off an assembly line and sent back in time to 1984.

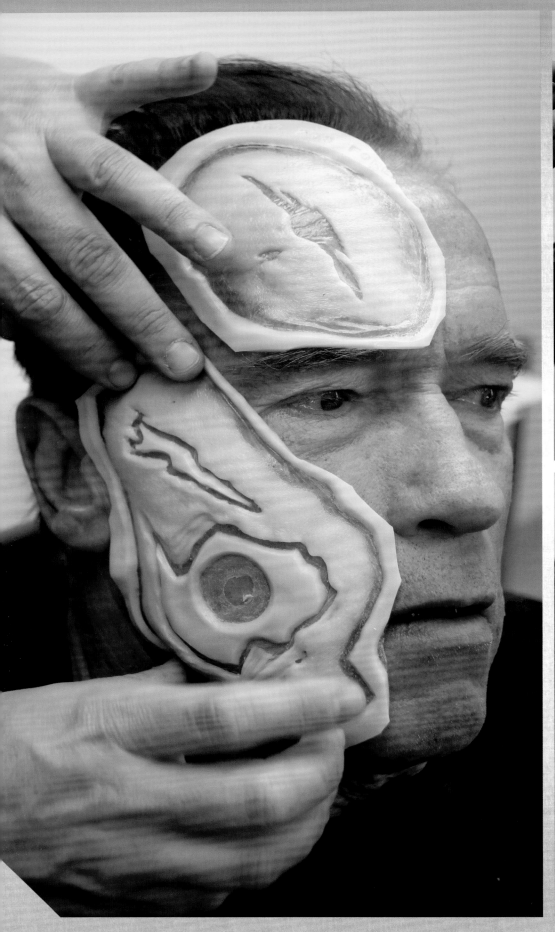

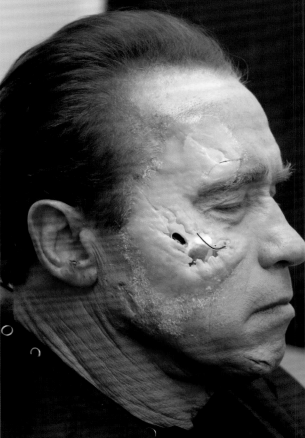

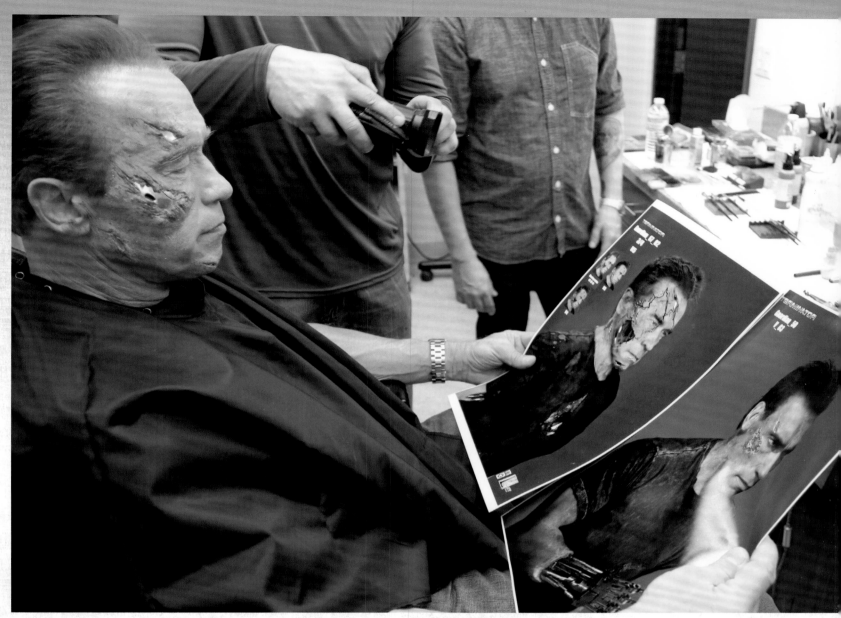

OPPOSITE: Legacy Effects makeup artists apply wound prosthetics to Arnold Schwarzenegger, showing Guardian's chrome endoskeleton. ABOVE: Schwarzenegger with the finished prosthetics and renderings of how the makeup will look in the final film. LEFT: The star poses with replicas of his legs taken from a cast made around thirty years ago. FOLLOWING PAGES: Legacy Effects also created a lifelike replica T-800 corpse that Guardian hauls around in *Terminator Genisys* based on casts of Schwarzenegger from the original film. Schwarzenegger inspected the model at the workshop and gave his approval.

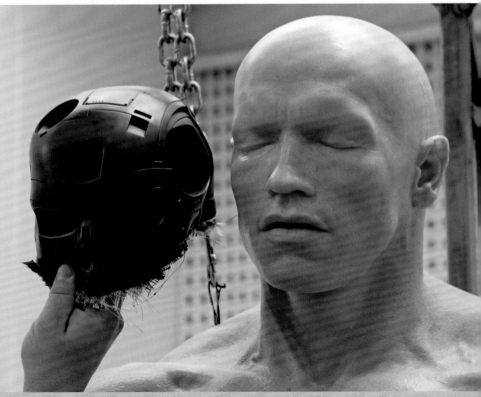

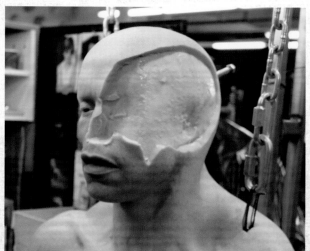

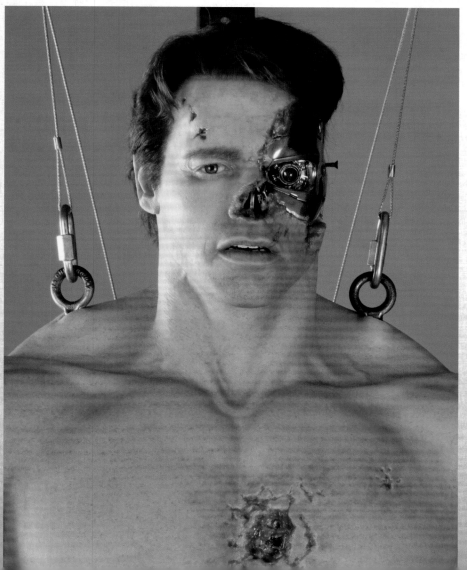

11

FIRE IN THE HOLE

WITH THE RISE OF DIGITAL VISUAL EFFECTS, "special effects" has taken on a specific meaning on film sets: the pyrotechnics, rigging, hydraulics, and other mechanical effects used to create effects that are photographed, not created on a computer. On *Terminator Genisys*, special effects ranged from the explosions of the Future War to a bus going airborne end-over-end, during a 2017 chase scene on the Golden Gate Bridge.

"Chase sequences are a signature piece of Terminator movies," says Ellison. "You don't find out that John Connor is the villain of our movie until late into the film. So we really wanted to ramp up all of the chase sequences that come after that to top anything that has come earlier in the movie. We wanted to show how strong John Connor as a terminator is, so you understand his superiority over Guardian later in the movie."

"BUT THE REAL CHALLENGE WAS THE SCENE INVOLVING THE SCHOOL BUS BEING TURNED OVER ON THE GOLDEN GATE BRIDGE."

So for the Golden Gate Bridge chase, he says, "We wanted to do something that you had never seen before." Ellison had loved the semi-truck flip in Christopher Nolan's *The Dark Knight*, which was shot with a real truck that really went end-over-end. "So we actually wanted to do one of the largest car flips you have ever seen," says Ellison, "and we wanted to do it entirely in camera."

Such effects take meticulous planning and testing. Once something is thoroughly planned and tested, shooting is just a matter of executing the plan, and usually that goes smoothly. But not always.

To prepare for the Future War sequence, special effects supervisor Mark Hawker ordered a massive amount of explosives: hundreds of pounds of black powder (which gives off a lot of smoke), 5,000 or 6,000 explosive squibs to simulate bullet hits, and hundreds of Kinepak explosive sticks. To simulate impacts from strafing runs, they'd use Nonel blasting caps. Taylor decreed the machines' plasma weapons in the Future War would cause purple explosions, so Hawker added purple fireworks to the mix.

But the real challenge was the scene involving the school bus being turned over on the Golden Gate Bridge. The bus was set to go end-over-end doing a 360-degree rotation and a twist in midair and land on its wheels pointing the other direction. Setting up the gag took four full

OPPOSITE: Arnold Schwarzenegger, Emilia Clarke, and Jai Courtney film a key sequence from the Golden Gate bridge scene.

weeks of prep and testing. Initially, the vehicle was to be a 20,000-pound city bus with nitrogen cannons built inside that would provide the force to flip it. "In the old days," Hawker explains, "they actually put a telephone pole inside of this steel tube with some black powder, and the powder was ignited—the force of that telephone pole being blasted out of the tube is what flipped the vehicle over." In a modern nitrogen cannon, compressed nitrogen replaces black powder, but the principle is the same.

The bus had three cannons, each with a six-foot piston. "These nitrogen cannons had 40,000 pounds of push on each one at the beginning of the push, and by time it got to the end, it was 30,000 pounds of push," says Hawker. "Multiply that by three, and it's, like, 'Yeah, the bus is definitely going to be going over.'"

The first test using the city bus was a success. The bus flipped end-over-end, rolled in midair, and landed on its wheels. "We were all excited," says Hawker. "Then I show it to David Ellison. He just thinks it's the coolest thing,

but then he goes, 'But can you make it turn over one more time?'"—in other words, skip the twist in midair and instead have the bus go end-over-end for a full 360 degrees, then land on its wheels facing the same direction as when it took off. That sent the dismayed Hawker back to the drawing board to recalculate. Fortunately for him and his special effects team, Taylor wanted to do the stunt with a school bus, which would be cheaper and 6,000 pounds lighter than a city bus. "On the day when we shot it, we didn't have time to do another test with the school bus. So we just went for it. Everything fortunately went really well."

For David Ellison, the stunt was a pinch-yourself moment: "Flipping a bus 360 degrees in the air . . . This was the kind of thing I used to dream about doing when I was a little kid playing with toy cars, but never in a million years did I think I would get the opportunity to actually do something like this."

ABOVE: Concept art shows Guardian trying to prevent the bus from toppling over the side of the Golden Gate Bridge. OPPOSITE BOTTOM: The bus flip stunt is one of the signature moments of *Terminator Genisys*.

101

12

GET ROLLING

PRINCIPAL PHOTOGRAPHY ON *TERMINATOR GENISYS* BEGAN on April 21, 2014. The jam-packed schedule had quite a few weeks when there was at least one unit working every day, which meant Taylor and some department heads could go weeks without a day off. "That is a true testament to everybody who worked on this movie," says David Ellison. "Everybody was willing to give up their nights, weekends, and, truly, their lives, for a time, to make this movie. I will always be grateful to our entire cast and crew for that."

First unit began mainly with 1984 sequences, which featured Schwarzenegger, Emilia Clarke, and Jai Courtney, as well as Byung-hun Lee as the T-1000, and J. K. Simmons as O'Brien. The second unit was mainly focused on the 2029 Future War sequences, which heavily featured Jason Clarke and Courtney, plus an appearance by former *Doctor Who* star Matt Smith playing one of the resistance fighters.

> "THE SCHEDULE WASN'T DRAWN UP WITH THE ACTORS IN MIND, BUT IT ALLOWED TAYLOR TO SHOOT THE STORY MORE OR LESS IN SEQUENCE FROM BEGINNING TO END . . . "

Taylor stayed with first unit, with accomplished second-unit director Alexander Witt overseeing the War. (Witt, who had a prior commitment to another film, had to depart *Terminator Genisys* during production. He was replaced by Brian Smrz, who Taylor calls "amazing.")

The schedule wasn't drawn up with the actors in mind, but it allowed Taylor to shoot the story more or less in sequence from beginning to end. However, with the Future War and 1984 exteriors up first, that meant shooting nights from April 21 through May 29. Nights can be very hard on the crew. "You kind of get discombobulated. It all becomes a blur," Susan Matheson explains. "You're trying to sleep in the day, but in the meantime, we're still fitting people in the daytime for scenes that are coming up. Then sometimes there are times that I'm working day and night. So it becomes very intense and very exciting." Alan Taylor actually began to enjoy it. "We would come back to New Orleans as the sun was coming up, and I would sit on my front stoop having a glass of wine as people went off to work. It was a completely vampire, topsy-turvy way to live."

RIGHT: Arnold Schwarzenegger poses for a wig test on the set. Guardian's hair varies from the rescue of Sarah in the 1970s to 1984 to 2017.

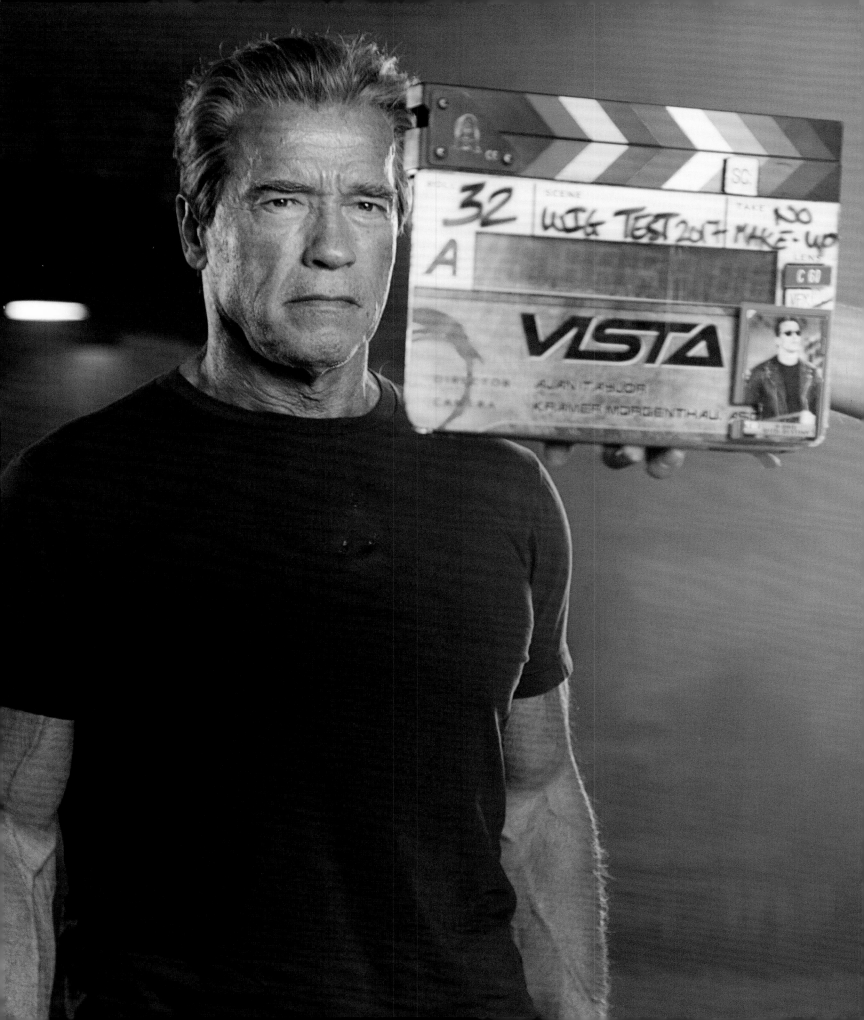

"and because everything is constantly in a state of change, you have to be sort of on tenterhooks, ready to react to whatever might come up."

Movie shoots are often carefully planned, but those plans also often have to change on the fly for any number of reasons, from bad weather to a sick cast member. The 1984 alley scene, where Reese arrives naked, was planned to differ from the original in a crucial way: Reese would find himself tangling with the T-1000. But the choreography for Jai Courtney and Byung-hun Lee had to change unexpectedly. "Jai picked the new choreography up right away," says Melissa Stubbs. "A lot of actors, you have to show them again and again, and you have to keep correcting them, like, 'Your hand is in the wrong position.' Jai would see it once and get it right away. And he really enjoyed it."

Taylor had his hands full directing such a massive production. Lee calls him "extremely smart" and "charismatic." "Every time I shared an idea with him, he would always listen and give a wise, thoughtful response. He speaks slowly and quietly, but whatever he would say would be the right thing," says Lee. J. K. Simmons had previously worked with Taylor on the HBO series *Oz* so knew what to expect: "I remembered him as a creative, efficient, funny, and all-around good guy. To be together again on a project of this magnitude, with all the moving parts and a very different pace, was really different, but at the end of the day, he handled all the disparate elements with the same alacrity and good humor I remembered."

Work continued around the clock. During daylight hours, the production office would be open; Mark Hawker's pyro crew would pack bombs and mortars with a mixture of cork and Gromulch to simulate earth and debris; props and armorers would prep guns and magazines; the costume team would launder the washable parts of the costumes and maintain the non-washable pieces, like the armor. Spisak and his builders would feverishly work to stay ahead of shooting and make sure both units had all the sets and props they needed for the next scenes on the schedule. "Nothing was ready until a day or two before we were going to shoot it," says Spisak,

With Taylor wrapped up in long days of shooting, the Skydance brain trust had to lend a hand. "We oftentimes had to do two- to three-hour meetings after wrap," says Ellison, "after we had shot a twelve, thirteen-hour day. So I was working seventeen, eighteen, sometimes twenty-hour days for pretty much the bulk of the shoot. And Alan had to go home and prepare for what he was shooting the next day." That left it to the producers to help out by planning for scenes that were still far off on the shooting schedule but had changed since pre-production.

The pace was relentless, and conditions were often uncomfortable, but people found ways to keep spirits high. Prop master Diana Burton enlisted the crew in a sweet search. Thinking that 2017 would have some food craze like the cronut, which was so trendy at the time of filming, she wondered: What would be the "donut of the future"? So every Friday the prop department brought in an assortment of treats from an excellent New Orleans shop, Southshore Donuts. "My personal favorite was the buttermilk donut," says Burton. "We polled the crew, and the red velvet donut was unanimously chosen as the donut of the future."

The makeup team, led by Lisa Love, made the care and comfort of the actors a top priority. Heat and humidity were a challenge during shooting, especially with actors wearing leather jackets and performing action scenes in steamy New Orleans. "When you're dying of sweat, it's nice to be cooled down," says Love. She came prepared with her own hand-made portable fans, which she builds from drill parts and even provided custom earplugs for actors and extras who would be near explosions and gunshots.

As terminators—albeit of very different models—Byung-hun Lee and Jason Clarke got a special airbrushed makeup treatment. "I wanted them to have a perfect-skin look," says Love, "and I took out a lot of the color from the skin. It was quite exciting." Clarke-as-John-Connor got two other makeup looks as well: When he's first seen fully human, he gets facial scars and some stippling for his stubble. When he appears for the first time as the T-3000, he's clean-shaven, although still bearing the scars. "It was just a little thing for the audience to go, 'Oh, there's something different about him,'" says Love. Finally, once his true nature is revealed, the scars disappear, and he gets the terminator skin treatment, a "flawless finish" with a lot of the red taken out of his skin tone.

OPPOSITE TOP: David Ellison and Dana Goldberg *(right)* look on as Jason Clarke and Byung-hun Lee discuss the art of playing a terminator. OPPOSITE BOTTOM AND BELOW: Director Alan Taylor at work on the set. Taylor, who has directed episodes of TV series *Game of Thrones* as well as Marvel's *Thor: The Dark World*, focused on the character dynamics amid the mayhem.

13

A DAY IN THE FUTURE WAR

THE FUTURE WAR HAD 300 EXTRAS, and each had unique makeup, props, and costumes. Each extra was assigned a number, so when he or she would report for work, the makeup artists, costumers, and prop crew would look up their numbers and outfit them accordingly. Extras had to be prepped hours before shooting started and then line up for review. Usually they would be found wanting in one respect: not dirty enough. Hair and makeup had custom "dirts" ready for their faces; costumers would add more dirt to their clothes. Night shooting meant extra dirt, so it would be apparent even in dim light. The effect was so transformative that Matheson would bump into some of the same people in the daytime and not recognize them.

> "THE WORKING PART OF THE SET EXPANDED INTO WHAT HAD ORIGINALLY BEEN THE 'CG ZONE'—THE AREA WHERE DIGITAL EFFECTS WERE SUPPOSED TO TAKE OVER AND NO PRACTICAL EFFECTS WERE SUPPOSED TO BE NECESSARY—AND THAT MEANT MORE EXPLOSIONS, MORE ACTION."

As the clock counted down to the first shot of the night, armorers checked gun barrels for lodged debris, ensuring nothing would fly out and cause injury when they were fired. The Future War had fifty working guns, and a typical single take used 3,000 rounds. One armorer was just tasked with changing magazines between takes. Some of Burton's plasma rifles were vehicle-mounted, and two more armorers were tasked with their care. The M134 Minigun, too, needed two armorers of its own.

Sequences would be altered during the night, so everyone had to be flexible. Hawker says his twenty-four-strong pyro crew "would basically wait for orders and then grab our steel traps that we use for pushing the debris and stuff in the air and just scramble. It was almost like a war zone in a way. You had to wait for your orders and then go out there and run and get things in position quick and be safe." The working part of the set expanded into what

OPPOSITE: John Connor fires his plasma cannon in a Future War battle scene. The scale of the Future War shoot exceeded even the ambitious plans of the stunt and pyrotechnics teams.

TOP AND OPPOSITE TOP: One hall-mark of Future War battle scenes: purple explosions echoing the purple of the plasma bolts. ABOVE: Kyle Reese cunningly commandeers a truck from the machines in order to infiltrate Skynet's work camp. OPPOSITE BOTTOM: Concept art shows the shattered and bleak Los Angeles following Judgment Day and the war with the machines.

had originally been the "CG zone"—the area where digital effects were supposed to take over and no practical effects were supposed to be necessary—and that meant more explosions, more action. Hawker ran through twice as much pyro as he'd budgeted for.

The makeup team tracked which extras had been near an explosion, jumping in to add cuts and blood to them

afterward. Love favored dark orange-red tones for fake blood. "I want the blood to be dark, but I want it to have a realness to it," she says. "Sometimes you'll want a bright blood if it's a very low-light situation. I do tend to go with the darker bloods, though."

Shooting would continue this way until the eastern sky began to lighten. Costumes were returned to wardrobe.

Weary performers and crew returned to their hotels, but the exhausted armorers lingered for two more hours, cleaning the guns assembly-line style and checking the "plasma rifle" shells for damage. "We'd be the only people left on the set," says Harry Lu. "It would get pretty lonely. The mosquitos start coming out just before the sun comes out. Your hands are covered with oil and grease, and you can't even scratch all your mosquito bites." By the time Lu's crew got to sleep, the production office would be opening, and the day crews would be getting to work. So it went for six weeks.

ABOVE: *Terminator Genisys* introduces Spider Tanks to the machines' arsenal. They're dropped into battle by flying Hunter-Killers like robot paratroops.
RIGHT: The resistance has its own war machines cobbled together from parts scavenged from the city's ruins.

14

A NIGHT IN LOS ANGELES

WHILE SECOND UNIT SHOT MOST OF THE FUTURE WAR, the first unit was hard at work capturing the 1984 scenes. That started with recreating the Griffith Park Observatory sequence from *The Terminator*, initially shot-for-shot and, at times, frame-for-frame. But when Guardian arrives to confront the T-800, the picture takes a sharp swerve.

"We knew this was going to be an iconic, central moment in the movie—the older Arnold facing down the younger Arnold," says Taylor. "So trying to do that justice and give it the weight it deserved was a big challenge."

Schwarzenegger's original T-800 terminator would ultimately be duplicated with visual effects, but a body double was needed for shooting. Finding a body double for Schwarzenegger's early '80s physique was no small matter; the actor's build at that time wasn't far from the peak condition he had been in when he won his Mr. Olympia titles. But as it happened, the filmmakers discovered there was a bodybuilder named Brett Azar who idolized Schwarzenegger and made it his goal to get his own body looking like Schwarzenegger's during his championship years. Azar was thrilled to "play" his hero, even if his role was essentially as a stand-in. He was given the flawless terminator makeup, then motion capture markers were applied all over his body, so he could be replaced with a digital double for Schwarzenegger in postproduction.

> **"WE KNEW THIS WAS GOING TO BE AN ICONIC, CENTRAL MOMENT IN THE MOVIE— THE OLDER ARNOLD FACING DOWN THE YOUNGER ARNOLD, SO TRYING TO DO THAT JUSTICE AND GIVE IT THE WEIGHT IT DESERVED WAS A BIG CHALLENGE."**

The night Schwarzenegger spoke his first lines on set was "electric and unbelievably cool," says David Ellison, talking about the scene at the Observatory where Guardian interrupts the T-800, and they square off: "You saw every single person revert back to the moment they saw

RIGHT: The out of commission T-800 created by Legacy Effects sits in the back of Sarah Connor's armored truck.

112

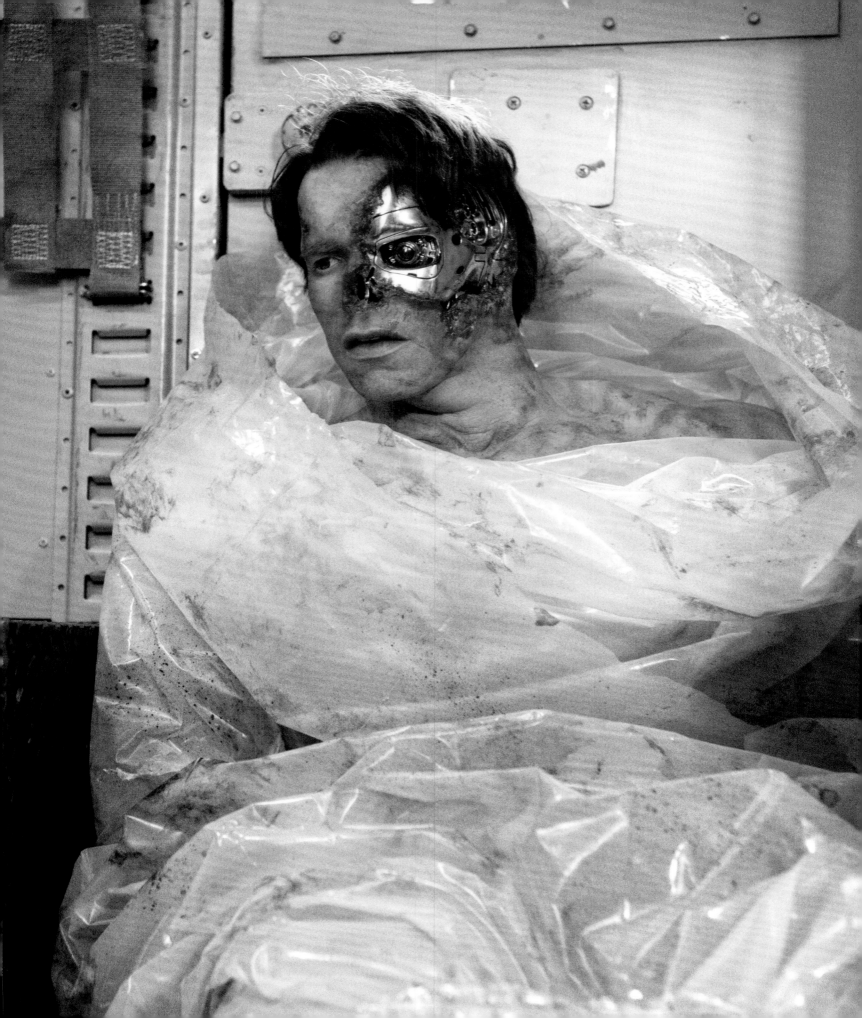

him in the theater for the very first time and become a little kid and just go 'Holy shit, the terminator's on set.'"

Of course, it wouldn't be a Terminator movie without Arnold Schwarzenegger saying his signature line, "I'll be back," a phrase he first uttered in *The Terminator*. The line came late in the script for *Terminator Genisys* during the helicopter chase above San Francisco. It was captured late in shooting as well, many weeks into the project. Schwarzenegger delivered the line twenty feet up in the air in a helicopter body attached to a gimbal, but when he said it, the crew broke into spontaneous applause. "It was 'My God, that's the moment! There it is!'" says Patrick Lussier.

Jai Courtney also had to re-create a scene from *The Terminator*: Kyle Reese breaking into a department store to get his pants, Nike Vandals, and military trench coat.

But in this version of the story, he's interrupted by a T-1000, a threat he hasn't prepared for and a terminator model he's never seen. Their gunfight in the department store didn't seem particularly dangerous compared with the wild action in other scenes, but Courtney suffered a shrapnel injury to his hand when a squib blew up early. That sent him to the emergency room and left him in a cast for a while. "That was a reminder early on," says Taylor, "that the threats are real when you're playing with something like this."

Reese is nearly killed by the T-1000 but is rescued by the woman he thought he had come to save, Sarah Connor, and Guardian, a terminator he thought he had come to fight. The fight with the T-1000 continues with a wild car chase through the streets, with Guardian behind the wheel of an armored truck. For a scene where the T-1000 is thrown

114

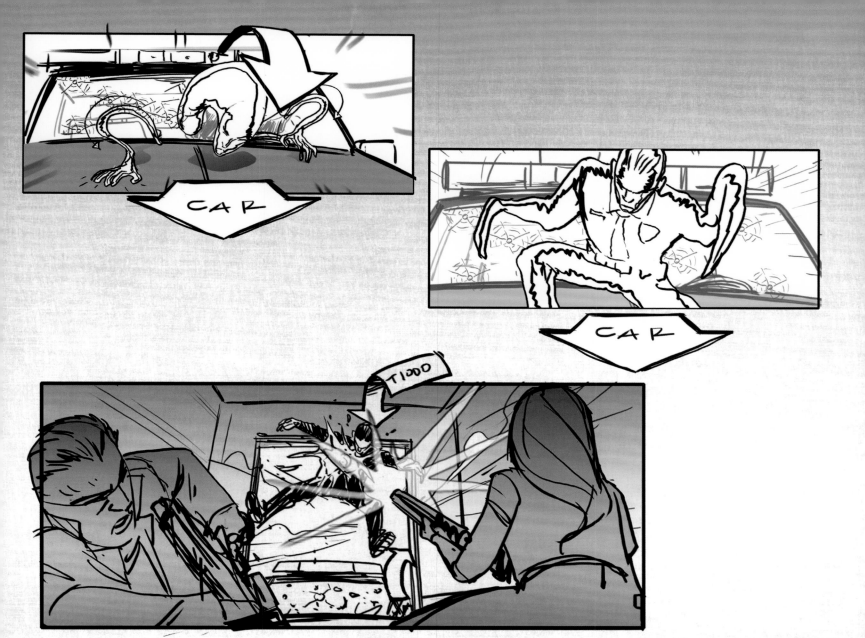

through the air to land on the roof of a car, it was required to land with the force of a 900-pound terminator, not a 200-pound man. So special effects supervisor Mark Hawker and his team were tasked with making the roof of the car implode at the very moment the stunt man landed on it. "We had to collapse the suspension, so we pulled the roof, the windshield, and everything down and crushed it as the stunt guy went into it," says Hawker. "We did that in one take. Which was fortunate because we only had one take to do it, but the timing on everything worked out really well."

Big stunts are meticulously planned, engineered, and tested. But there are things no one thinks to test, things that, if they fail, don't necessarily pose a danger to life and limb but threaten the schedule, budget, and everyone's sanity. Things like . . . doors.

PUNK 1 : NICE NIGHT FOR A WALK , EH?

"We had a problem with doors," admits Dana Goldberg. "Doors didn't work in our movie every once in a while." In fact, uncooperative doors became a punch line on the set.

In the armored truck chase, the script called for Sarah to throw open the truck doors, say "Come with me if you want to live," and reveal Guardian. "The first six times the door would open halfway," says Ellison. "We were, like, this is getting really old." "The damn doors were cursed," laughs Emilia Clarke. "It was ridiculous. Absolutely insane." In another scene, the script called for Guardian to punch a

door open. It was a simple breakaway door, with two backups in case something went wrong. On the first take, the wire on the door broke. On the second take, it only bent partway. Luckily, the third door worked perfectly. In one of the Time Displacement Device scenes, the doors failed and held up shooting for four hours. "We actually did at some point say we should call this movie *Terminator: Doors*," says Goldberg.

Schwarzenegger made his presence felt both on- and off-screen. Ellison says, "Arnold is a phenomenal leader and partner on set and really does the amazing thing that only

OPPOSITE TOP AND LEFT: Guardian's entrance is a new twist on the Griffith Park Observatory sequence in the first Terminator film. Re-creating the punks was hard, but finding a body double for a young Arnold Schwarzenegger was even harder. BELOW: Storyboards for Guardian's entrance and the beginning of his fight with the T-800.

a movie star like him can do, which is really inspire the best in everybody around him." Schwarzenegger would remind everyone that *The Terminator* and *T2* had pushed the limits of action and visual effects and that *Terminator Genisys* must do the same. "He was constantly pushing for 'What are we going to do with our new terminator in this movie that gives the audience the same I've-never-seen-that-before effect you got when you saw *Terminator 2: Judgment Day*?'" says Ellison.

When it came to action, says Ellison, Schwarzenegger reminded everyone that gunplay gets old quickly in a Terminator film, because "ultimately guns are very ineffective against terminators," says Ellison, "and a great terminator action sequence requires using vehicles and your surrounding environment as weapons."

With stunts, Schwarzenegger pushed for bigger and better. "At times, when he felt like it wasn't there," says Ellison, "he would say things like, 'I've done that stunt before! Why are we doing it in this movie? This needs to be better. We did this in *T2*. Let's not repeat it.' Arnold really does have that dedication to doing things himself and to constantly push the bar to do what nobody else will."

Schwarzenegger also reminded the company that heart and humor are essential parts of the best Terminator films. The characters would need to be three-dimensional and emotional. "He would oftentimes talk about the additional photography they did on *T2* to get the audience to the payoff moment where they cry when the terminator is lowered into the steel," says Ellison. He also reminded them that *T2* has great one-liners and some very funny moments, and he worked hard to make sure those comic moments landed.

Schwarzenegger wasn't known as a comic actor when he first played the terminator, but in the years since he has demonstrated a knack for comedy, excelling in the likes of *Kindergarten Cop* and *Twins*. Not only did he land the comic moments in *Terminator Genisys*, he proved a bit of a cut-up. Emilia Clarke says, "You'd kind of be doing the scene, and they'd yell 'Cut!' and right on cue everyone would be in stitches because of what he was doing. To have an iconic figure like that that everyone's grown up admiring, having him crack a joke is just wonderful."

Away from the cameras, Schwarzenegger became a favorite with cast and crew alike. "Arnold is about as iconic as

it gets, of course," says J. K. Simmons, "and I was really glad to see what a nice, approachable guy he is." Each day the star would settle outside his trailer, light up a cigar, and surround himself with people. "Sometimes I'd just be walking by, and he'd say 'Come here! Come talk to me!'" says Susan Matheson. "He definitely has a joie de vivre. He loves life, and I think he loves all people." Diana Burton adds, "If Arnold was around, the set always was a happier place."

The Terminator films were seen around the world, and Byung-hun Lee grew up watching them—and Schwarzenegger. "When I was a kid, after winning the arm wrestling championship at my school, I was given the nickname 'Terminator,'" says Lee. "That nickname oddly stuck with me for years. Filming with Arnold on the set of the newest Terminator movie was one of the most surreal experiences of my life."

Patrick Lussier remembers a day when Arnold told Jai Courtney, "You're in very good shape."

"Jai was, like, 'Arnold said I'm in good shape!'" says Lussier. "He was thrilled by that."

"And who wouldn't be?" adds Kalogridis.

15

SOARING THROUGH SAN FRANCISCO

THOUGH A LARGE SECTION OF *TERMINATOR GENISYS* is set in San Francisco, New Orleans plays San Francisco for much of the 2017 sequences. It was NOLA residents, not San Franciscans, who tolerated a freeway shutdown for the filming of Sarah and Reese's arrival. Likewise, the Golden Gate Bridge scenes were shot in Louisiana, not California, on a replica comprising some 500 feet of faux Golden Gate. Five hundred feet proved surprisingly limiting for car chase shots, only enough for six-second takes, but it was ample for the end-over-end bus stunt.

Once that gag was done, though, the script called for another daunting sequence: The bus was to dangle vertically off the side of the Golden Gate Bridge while the characters tried to clamber to safety, all the while avoiding the T-3000. To hang or not to hang: That was the question. The bus could be hung vertically for real, but tests showed that it really wasn't necessary. On camera, the bus could be flat on the ground on its wheels but would appear to be vertical—if the camera was turned sideways. But the actors couldn't climb from one end of the bus to the other if the bus was horizontal. The question was: make it easier on the camera unit with a horizontal bus or on the stunt unit with a vertical bus? The camera team and the horizontal bus won out. The stunt team had to cut slots in the roof of the bus, rig the actors with wires and harnesses, and puppeteer them, so they would appear to be climbing to safety. The sequence took three days to shoot, with stars Emilia Clarke, Jai Courtney, and Jason Clarke in the bus almost all the time. "I don't think Jai ever got out of his harness," says Melissa Stubbs, "and he never complained. I would have been out of that thing in thirty minutes."

The 2017 action includes a helicopter chase between buildings in the streets of San Francisco as the heroes race to Cyberdyne headquarters to head off the birth of Skynet.

> "THE BUS WAS TO DANGLE VERTICALLY OFF THE SIDE OF THE GOLDEN GATE BRIDGE WHILE THE CHARACTERS TRIED TO CLAMBER TO SAFETY, ALL THE WHILE AVOIDING THE T-3000. "

RIGHT: Wirework is used to shoot the interior of the dangling bus as Jai Courtney's Kyle Reese hangs on for dear life.

This couldn't be achieved with real aircraft, as helicopters aren't permitted to fly so close to the ground in the city. As a result, the visual effects team had to build a virtual San Francisco to serve as the background for the chase. Meanwhile, for shots featuring the actors, helicopter chassis were placed on gimbals that could rock the facsimile vehicles back and forth, simulating the violent motion of the chase scenes. Or, for an action beat where the helicopter is taking off, the filmmakers would utilize a "poor man's gimbal," as Hawker calls it: a long-reach forklift attached to a helicopter body where the rotor would normally be.

"It was a logistical bear to shoot," says Taylor, "because you're shooting gimbaled helicopter bodies against green screen and adding that into a plate you shoot in San Francisco. Trying to make it all feel photo-real and energized is tricky."

The film's final action sequence in the server maze inside Cyberdyne headquarters was filmed on a relatively small set. It was originally planned to be a digital-only set consisting of green screens, but late in production it was decided to build part of it for real. The set had lights built into it and digital extensions that in the final film make it appear to continue out almost to infinity. "That allows for a certain efficiency," says Taylor, "especially if it's going to be looking the same almost no matter what angle you see it from." For the chase through the maze, the actors could do a short take that ended with them running around the corner. Then in the next take they could run to the same spot they'd just left. "You keep using the same real estate over and over again," says Taylor. "It's a trick we use a lot."

ABOVE: A shot of the Golden Gate Bridge rescue scene with the digital background completed. OPPOSITE BOTTOM LEFT: Guardian finds himself in a tight spot.

ABOVE: Concept art depicts the arrival of our heroes at Cyberdyne headquarters following a midair helicopter chase with the T-3000. LEFT: Live-action shooting of the sequence involved use of blue screen and a movable helicopter chassis.

The server maze was shot near the end of production in New Orleans before shooting moved to San Francisco for exterior work. The set also featured not one, not two, but four sets of doors. Dana Goldberg recalls Emilia Clarke in rehearsal saying, "Four sets of doors? We're totally screwed." But on the first take, all the doors worked perfectly, and Clarke shouted, "The doors showed up! Let's hear it for the doors!" Cast and crew gave the doors a standing ovation.

Shooting wrapped at the beginning of August in San Francisco, and it was an emotional time for cast and crew alike. Some, like John Rosengrant and Harry Lu, had revisited a franchise that had helped launch their careers. For others, like Susan Matheson, the very chance to work on the film had been a dream come true. "As designers, I think we always wish for moments like this," says Matheson, "but often these moments don't come. To be given the opportunity to work on something that you've felt passionate about for so long . . . it's an extraordinary experience."

Jai Courtney had shot his largest movie role yet alongside one of his idols. "I mean, a Terminator movie—it doesn't really get better than that," he says. "Without Arnie, it just would have never been what it was. He is that franchise. And to have him back, it's just really cool to be a part of."

With photography complete, the action shifted to workstations, screening rooms, and recording stages around the world, as the editorial, sound, and digital effects teams took center stage.

OPPOSITE TOP: Concept art shows Sarah Connor and Kyle Reese running through the corridors of Cyberdyne headquarters as the battle to determine the future begins. OPPOSITE BOTTOM: Concept art shows the detail that went into creating the various components of the server room. TOP: Director Alan Taylor on the Cyberdyne HQ set. ABOVE: The server maze proved to be one of the most striking *Terminator Genisys* sets.

PART 4 | DISPLACING TIME
(VISUAL EFFECTS & SOUND)

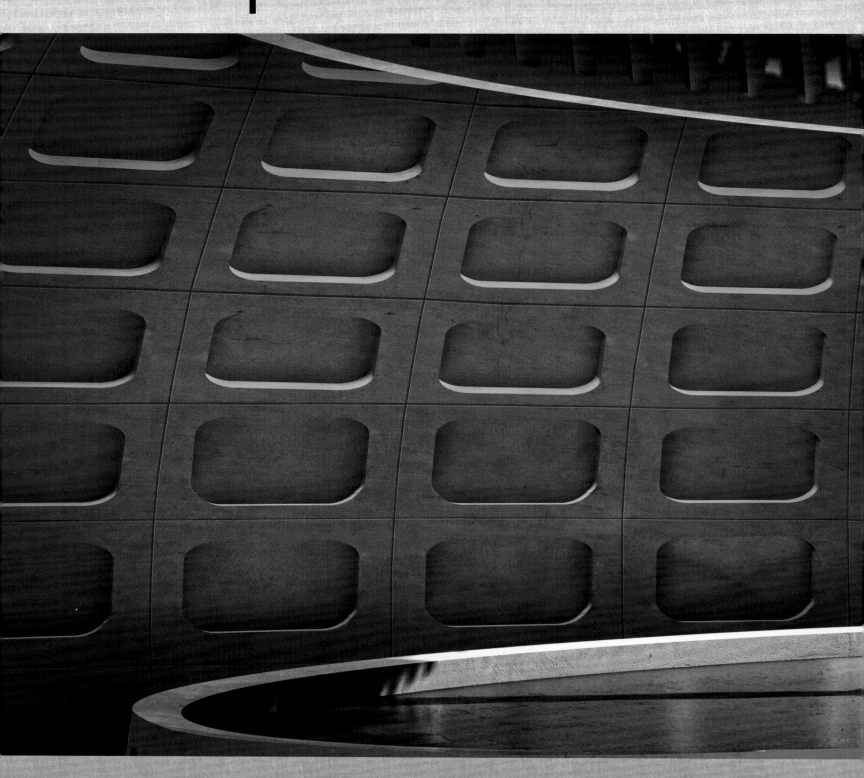

16

UPGRADING THE FUTURE

SO MANY ELEMENTS OF *TERMINATOR GENISYS* would be familiar to audiences: Sarah, Reese, Schwarzenegger's terminator (as both hero and villain), the liquid metal T-1000, and, to a lesser degree, John Connor. But the Terminator mythos was spawned thirty years ago, so, in *Terminator Genisys*, the filmmakers felt it was time to build upon each of these iconic aspects of the saga. "Everything is about getting an upgrade," says visual effects producer Shari Hanson. "The time-travel sphere gets an upgrade. Arnold gets an upgrade. John Connor is an upgrade. The T-1000 gets an upgrade. Even our endoskeletons got an upgrade."

Hanson came onto the picture as the first hire for the visual effects team. She had worked with Paramount on several projects, including Michael Bay's first *Transformers* film, J. J. Abrams's *Star Trek* reboot, and Gore Verbinski's animated western *Rango*. Asked to help ensure the new Terminator had eye-catching visuals, she was tasked with creating what she calls: "key moments that were groundbreaking, unique, never been done before."

> ## "EVERYTHING IS ABOUT GETTING AN UPGRADE. THE TIME-TRAVEL SPHERE GETS AN UPGRADE. ARNOLD GETS AN UPGRADE. JOHN CONNOR IS AN UPGRADE. THE T-1000 GETS AN UPGRADE. EVEN OUR ENDOSKELETONS GOT AN UPGRADE."

Visual effects pros are so often asked to provide "something we've never seen before" that it's become a running joke in their business. In the case of *Terminator Genisys*, though, there were three obvious opportunities for never-before-seen effects: the digitally youthful Arnold Schwarzenegger "synthespian," the Schwarzenegger vs. Schwarzenegger fight scene, and the new T-3000 that would be the film's main villain.

But it's still not easy to break new ground in visual effects. On the contrary, believable digital humans have been tantalizingly out of reach for some time. "Whenever you say, 'There are multiple things you do in this movie that have never been done before,'" admits

OPPOSITE: An early concept for the T-3000's transformation process shows it forming a whiplike weapon with its right arm.

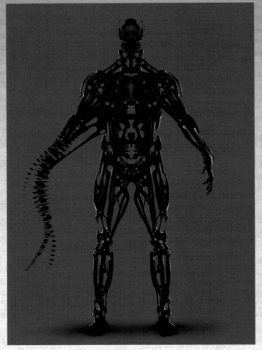

Ellison, "they sound really good when you first say them and then reality leads to banging your head against the wall as you try to achieve them."

In November 2013, Janek Sirrs came on board as visual effects supervisor, joining Hanson to oversee the numerous visual effects companies that would execute the visual effects. Sirrs is a veteran of numerous "tentpole" films, including *The Avengers* and *Batman Begins*. Coming on just a few months before the start of shooting, Sirrs was soon racing against the clock. Visual effects is usually considered postproduction, but in the era of digital filmmaking, visual effects planning typically begins before the first shot is captured, and shot production continues until just weeks before release.

Visual effects studios began pitching for the film around the time Sirrs was hired and were soon delivering test shots. London-based Double Negative (DNeg), director Christopher Nolan's visual effects studio of choice, was keen to create the T-3000. "We desperately wanted to try to get a project of that caliber into the facility," says DNeg's visual effects supervisor Peter Bebb. "We had a rough brief: 'Create an iconic terminator character. The technology is nano.' But that was pretty much it." With that minimal guidance, DNeg put together a test shot, showing their concept terminator getting shot, reacting, then reassembling. Handing in the test in January 2014, they were awarded the assignment of creating the T-3000 in April just before shooting started. Bebb journeyed to New Orleans to begin the on-set visual effects planning.

Meanwhile, Technicolor's visual effects subsidiary, Moving Picture Company (MPC), secured the contract to work on much of the Future War and Observatory sequences, including the critical Schwarzenegger "synthespian."

Bebb estimates DNeg alone probably created 800 to 1,000 digital effects shots in *Terminator Genisys*. How much has the world changed since *T2*? Legacy Effects' John Rosengrant estimates that on that film there were probably only forty to sixty fully digital effects shots.

Digital effects can seem like a technical process and do indeed require highly advanced technology, but at heart their creation remains an artistic endeavor, not a technical one. Creating the new models of terminator in the latest film, says Sirrs, begins with the story and characters. "What will the nature of this terminator be? What drives it? What does it need to do?" he explains. "How they get portrayed visually springs out of that. So you start plundering the story." The visual effects team even compiles a list of adjectives and nouns that fit the digital character's motivation. Then they collect hundreds of images that evoke those ideas. "You cull sources, and you hope that out of this big collection of sources of material—whether it be adjectives, pictures, or movies—you see little aspects where you go, 'Ah, OK, I can see a glimmer there that is applicable to this character.'" Eventually that art is presented to the director and producers—the "grown-ups," Sirrs calls them—for approval.

In the case of *Terminator Genisys*, there was the extra challenge of designing for a trilogy. Some effects, such as the T-5000 that appears late in the film, would be introduced with an eye toward appearances in the second and third installments, so they required as much design as a "hero" effect like the T-3000.

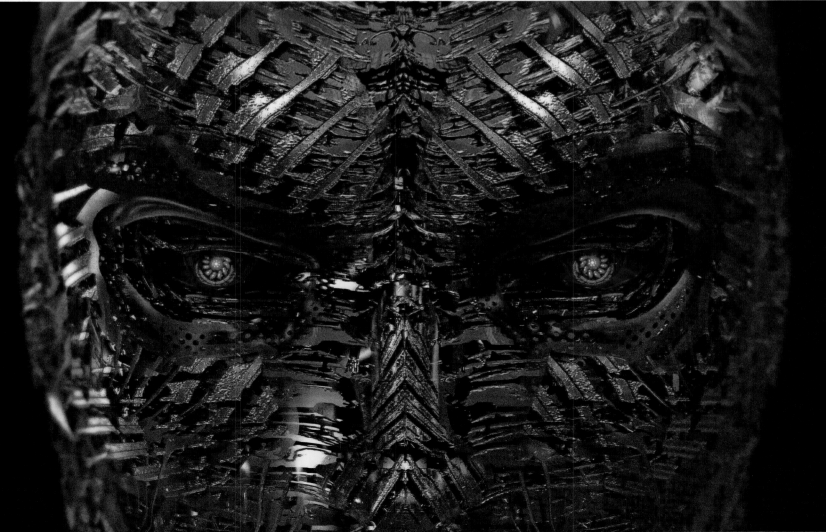

TOP: Concept art explores how the T-3000 might react to being shot through its abdomen. ABOVE AND LEFT: Early VFX concepts show how the T-3000 might use its changeable mass to wreak havoc on the Golden Gate Bridge. OPPOSITE: Further concept illustrations for the T-3000's endoskeleton.

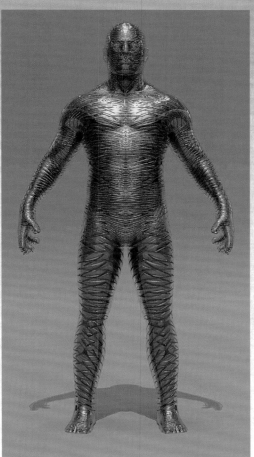
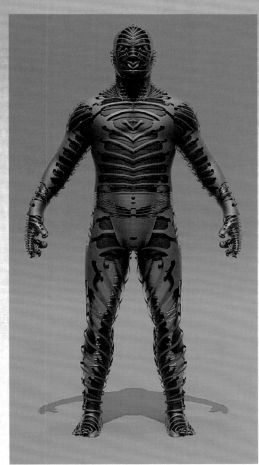
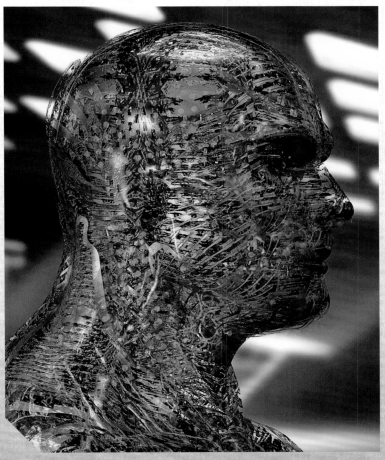

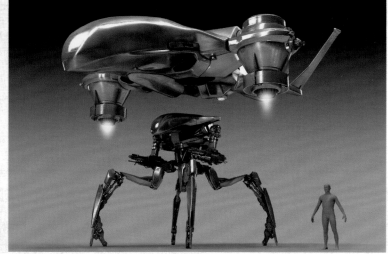

The Future War sequence was always expected to rely heavily on visual effects, but Hanson calls the sequence "extraordinarily difficult." First, it featured a crucial moment in the Terminator mythos—when Reese and John Connor finally beat down the machines and discover the Time Displacement Device—that had never been depicted on-screen before, so fans would have high expectations. Second, despite the enormous effort that was put into shooting the Future War, the visual effects team would have to add enormous scope and scale to the battle. The battle scenes had flying Hunter-Killers, Spider Tanks, helicopters, and armies of resistance fighters, plus thousands of T-800 endoskeletons, fighting on a battlefield miles across, all of which would have to be created digitally. "You're taking the part that was filmed," says Hanson, "and it's a postage stamp

in a shot that's actually a hundred times larger."

MPC's visual effects supervisor, Sheldon Stopsack, oversaw the creation of the Spider Tanks, a new weapon in the machines' arsenal. "A Spider Tank is a four-legged robotic machine that acts more like an advanced ground troop," he says. "It is certainly bigger than the endoskeleton, certainly more complex in terms of its firepower and its size and its agility." Spider Tanks are actually integrated into the familiar, flying Hunter-Killers that were introduced in *The Terminator*. "Certain Hunter-Killers have a Spider Tank mounted on the belly as part of their armor basically and are able to drop these wherever needed to get them engaged into the ground battle."

In the Future War battle, the Hunter-Killers engage a fleet of helicopters piloted by the resistance. In a full-on

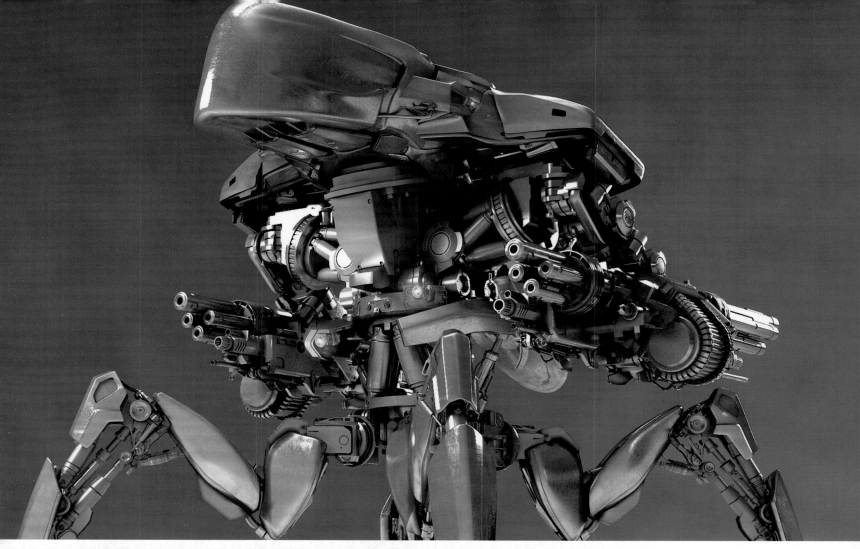

OPPOSITE PAGE: Concept art shows the deployment of a Spider Tank by a Hunter-Killer. ABOVE: Detail of a Spider Tank; note the signature glowing red eyes associated with Skynet technology. LEFT: Various designs for the airborne Hunter-Killer robots.

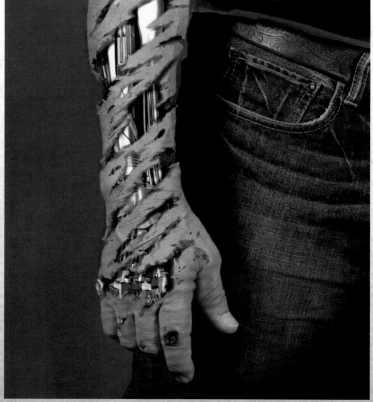

war movie, the production might have paid to rent those helicopters or at least some of them. But for a single scene, it made more sense to let the visual effects team add both the helicopters and the Hunter-Killers.

Another piece of the film that relies heavily on visual effects is Reese's dream sequences and split memories. Reese's journey back from 2029 to 1984 puts him in a paradoxical spot: He arrives in the past with memories of two timelines, one he recognizes and one he doesn't. "The challenge there was to communicate the sort of ripping apart of one's consciousness," says Sirrs. "What was one person's memory is now being forked, and we are seeing two competing things lodged in his brain." Reese himself doesn't understand the new memories, but in time they prove crucial for understanding how his mission to the past has evolved.

Besides the Future War, Moving Picture Company also had to make it possible for Arnold Schwarzenegger to appear in *Terminator Genisys* as he did in 1984. Complete success for that alone would be groundbreaking, but the Observatory sequence demanded even more digital magic. The T-800 that arrives at the start of the sequence looks as Schwarzenegger did in the early 1980s. Guardian, the terminator that fights him, is older but only appears to be in his fifties—about the same age Schwarzenegger was in *Terminator 3: Rise of the Machines*. So it would be an all-digital Schwarzenegger versus a live action-but-digitally-youthened Schwarzenegger, all shot on a set in Louisiana with a digital Los Angeles background that would be added in post.

Sirrs says that while the initial portions of the 1984 portion of the film needed to evoke the original movie, the need for such mimicry fades as the film progresses. "You can allow yourself to drift away into more modern sensibilities once you've settled into the scene," he says.

But putting a convincing all-digital Schwarzenegger terminator into the recreated Observatory sequence is "probably the biggest challenge you can even face in visual effects at the moment," says MPC's Stopsack, "because it's such a known character and such a known sequence, and everyone really knows what Arnold looked like at that time, and people have a clear idea of what it needs to look like."

There are proven cheats for filmmakers who want to hide flaws in their visual effects: Keep the monster in the dark or in bad weather, and keep the camera at a distance. And it helps if your creature is something people haven't seen in real life, so they don't have a frame of reference.

But in this sequence, says Alan Taylor, those cheats were mostly off the table. "This one is at a level of scrutiny that is daunting," he says. "He will be shot in close-up. He is absolutely human. The margin of error is zero." Creating a convincing digital Schwarzenegger would be even harder than creating a character from scratch, precisely because Schwarzenegger is so famous.

Ellison understood going in that creating a completely believable digital double for Arnold Schwarzenegger would mean going beyond any synthespian ever created. "In the past," says Ellison, "you'd get a dead-behind-the-eyes thing. You'd get

OPPOSITE TOP LEFT: Digital art created by Legacy Effects shows a battle-damaged Guardian with his endoskeleton exposed from the forearm down. These studies helped to determine how the effect would be accomplished in the final film. OPPOSITE BOTTOM LEFT: Another Legacy Effects rendering show Guardian's arm with fragments of flesh stripped off. OPPOSITE RIGHT: A detailed study of Guardian's damaged arms shows flesh and ligaments still attached to his metal endoskeleton. BELOW: Digital renders for the battle-damaged head of the T-800 that Guardian takes down in 1984.

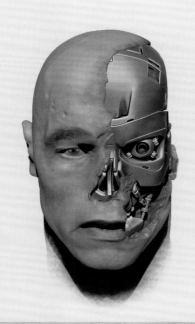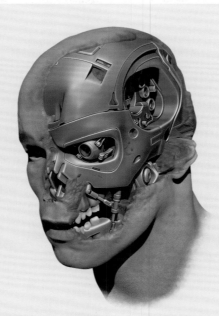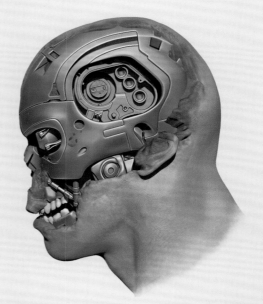

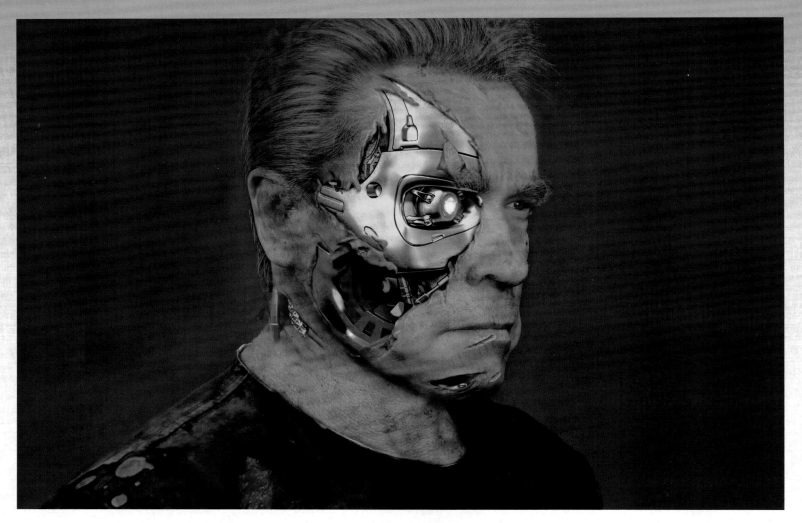

a rubbery skin that you don't believe and doesn't feel porous, and the way light reflects off the glistening of somebody's eyes [would be unrealistic]—there's a thousand little things . . ."

Stopsack says the struggle to get from 95 percent to 100 percent "there" on a digital human can drive a visual effects artist to distraction, so the visual effects supervisors must plan what steps should be taken and in what order. "If there's just the slightest sort of discrepancy, the audience won't buy it," says Stopsack. "It gets to that point where, for an artist or even as a supervisor, it becomes hard to determine what is actually wrong with it. You find yourself in a desperate situation all of a sudden, where you don't really know what is actually the right thing to do."

The digital double for the young Schwarzenegger is built for "every shot possible," says Sirrs, meaning any angle and even extreme close-ups. "Luckily," says Hanson, "Mr. Schwarzenegger is one of the most heavily documented individuals there is. And James Cameron was a very early adopter of technology and so we have some of his first cyber scans and a lot of life casts from Legacy Effects of Arnold from ages thirty-five to now sixty-seven." Due to this archive

ABOVE: Studies like this were essential in planning which part of Arnold Schwarzenegger's face would have to be covered with green screen patches during filming so that digital damage could later be added. OPPOSITE TOP: Digital renders of Guardian's damaged face. OPPOSITE BOTTOM: A design concept depicts a moment when, in an echo of the original film, Guardian is cut in half but the upper half of his body fights on.

of reference material, there's no shortage of information on *exactly* what Arnold looked like at various stages in his life.

Hard as it would be to make the digital double look exactly like the Schwarzenegger of 1984, that wouldn't be enough; it would have to *act* like Schwarzenegger. So the visual effects team returned to Schwarzenegger's films of that era—including *The Terminator*, of course—to study his expressions, mannerisms, and acting choices, so their digital Schwarzenegger would perform as he might have done then, not as he does today. But even within those strictures, there was some room for the visual effects team to take some creative license. Sirrs says that people tend to mentally combine Schwarzenegger's performances in the first two Terminator films, so their synthespian will be a hybrid of the two.

Meanwhile Legacy Effects combined some old and new ideas for moments when the Schwarzenegger terminators (Guardian and the killer T-800) suffer wounds that reveal their endoskeletons. The endoskeleton from *The Terminator* had been designed to fit within Schwarzenegger's real-life physique. Legacy still had all its measurements, as well as life casts of Schwarzenegger.

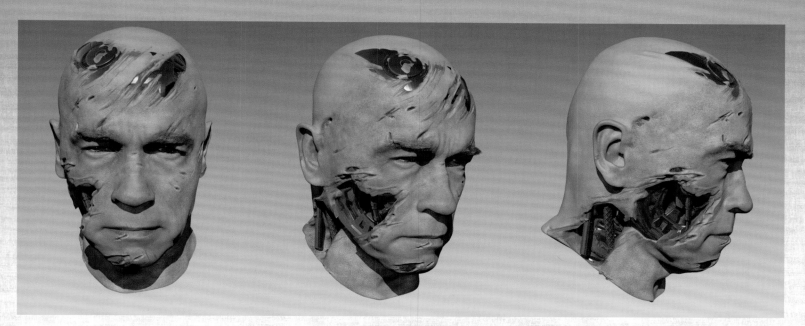

Therefore, for the T-800 circa 1984 and for Guardian, they were able to create a digital Schwarzenegger of their own, then put a digital model of the endoskeleton inside it. So for prosthetic wounds that had been painted with the green-screen color on set, they needed only to line up their digital Arnold-with-a-chrome-skeleton model to reveal exactly the right bit of mechanism that should be visible through the wound in the final film.

The 2017 sequences meant creating a digital Golden Gate Bridge. The Golden Gate has been rendered digitally in numerous films, but there's no digital rental house with this famous landmark ready on demand; software changes too quickly, so each film ends up building it from scratch. And, as often as it's done, there's always something new to discover. The bridge has a lot of details that aren't obvious, but if they're missing, it won't look right. "There's how the road cracks," says Sirrs, "and there's chewing gum marks on sidewalks, and things all over the place that accumulate over the years. You look at the CG bridge and then at the real one and you're, like, 'Yup, it's missing that.'"

The bridge is just part of a vast virtual San Francisco that had to be created for the action scenes, especially for the helicopter chase. Says Hanson, "We spent a month in the city walking up and down streets. We shot from fifty-seven rooftops and captured entire buildings. We shot six days a week for a month shooting plates for that sequence." The photos would eventually comprise ten terabytes of data, and it was enough to build a 3-D, digital San Francisco to be navigated by virtual helicopters.

SOUND DESIGN

Sound designer Ethan Van der Ryn is among those coming full circle with *Terminator Genisys*; his first credit was as a sound effects assistant on *Terminator 2: Judgment Day*. "It was a real cathartic and seminal experience," he says of the earlier film. "It's interesting and fun for me to go back into that same world and take up where I left off all those years ago."

Van der Ryn drew inspiration from the sound design of the original two Terminator films, especially *T2*, while taking advantage of the capabilities of digital sound software that wasn't available then. His first step in sound design is to ground the sometimes fantastical images on the screen in reality. "Sound is a crazily powerful tool for doing that," he says. "If we can ground it in a visceral reality, it allows us to believe it, and once we believe it, we'll go anywhere with it." For example, for the flying Hunter-Killer robots in the future scenes, his team recorded the sound of an airplane turbine

and "bent" it with Pro Tools. "So it's something that feels familiar, but we've never quite heard before," he says.

Then he looks to add emotion to the sound effects. On *Terminator Genisys*, that often means giving the machines a soulful sound: "That's about playing with natural sounds that feel like they're bridging the gap between the machine and living world, because that's what's so interesting about this world: They're machines, but they're also living in a way." The motors of a Spider Tank, for example, have a "vocal-ish" sound that gives them personality. "Tonally, it's important to hit the sweet spot between not enough soul and spirit and too much. I think that sweet spot exists, and when you hit it, you know that it feels right."

While visual effects artists can use digital tools to create photo-realistic images, there's been no such digital revolution in sound. Sound editors like Van der Ryn still

ABOVE AND OPPOSITE: Sound was a hugely important part of the *Terminator Genisys* shoot and postproduction process.

create effects by making sounds and recording them. For the Spider Tanks' guns, for example, his team bent 20 feet of quarter-inch copper tubing into a spring-like coil, then tapped on it, and recorded the sound.

For the squelching, liquid sound that accompanies the T-1000's morphing abilities, Van der Ryn is truly going old school, but with a *Terminator Genisys* upgrade.

"On *Terminator 2*, Gary Rydstrom used the sound of his dog's food sliding out of its metal can—micing that very closely—for the main component of the T-1000's

suction-y sound." So for *Terminator Genisys*, the sound assistants made a shopping run to get every canned food product in every size that they could find. "We put down a plastic mat inside our recording room and did a massive recording session where they recorded all these different jams, jellies, and whatnot sliding out of cans," says Van der Ryn. "So we've been using that to come up with a whole new palette of T-1000 sounds that will relate back to the original sounds."

17

THE TERMINATORS

WHAT WOULD A TERMINATOR MOVIE BE without those malevolent, lethal infiltration units, the eponymous terminators? *Terminator Genisys* brings back old favorites from *The Terminator* and *Terminator 2: Judgement Day*, gives them a twenty-first-century makeover, and then delivers two entirely new terminator concepts for good measure.

T-800

The T-800 endoskeleton, first seen on-screen after the fiery tanker truck crash in *The Terminator*, is too iconic to change drastically. But nothing is ever perfect.

The original "Endos" proportions allowed stop-motion animators to manipulate a miniature puppet version of it easily, a technique that's no longer used to bring these automatons to life. The new Endo is sleeker, says Legacy's John Rosengrant, and has a matte finish, unlike the polished chrome of the original. "An interesting thing used to happen with the terminator," says Rosengrant. "You'd have to put dulling spray on it because it was so damn bright. You'd see the whole camera crew's reflection in the shot every time." The new Endo also gets some darker-colored components, so it looks like it is made of more than one material. "The design is a little less chunky," says Rosengrant. "It's more finessed."

> **"THERE'S 145 PARTS OR MORE ON THE TERMINATOR. EVERY ONE OF THEM HAS TO BE HAND-CRAFTED AND MOLDED AND ASSEMBLED. SO IT'S STILL A VERY HANDS-ON, INTRICATE ART THAT WE DO."**

Most of the Endos on-screen will be CG, but Legacy Effects still had to build a full-sized Endo for some scenes, notably an early Future War shot where an Endo drives the truck that carries Reese and other resistance fighters into the work camp. Legacy went from concept drawings to shipping its finished, life-sized Endo model in just four months. "The days of working on something for a year and a half, those are long gone," says Rosengrant. After the art department provided the new design, Legacy 3D-printed prototype parts, made silicone molds for each, and used those molds to cast plastic copies. "There's 145 parts or more on the terminator," says Rosengrant. "Every one of them has to be

RIGHT: Revisions to the T-800 from *Terminator Genisys* include a differently shaped skull and different colors and finishes for various metal components, but the menacing red eyes remain.

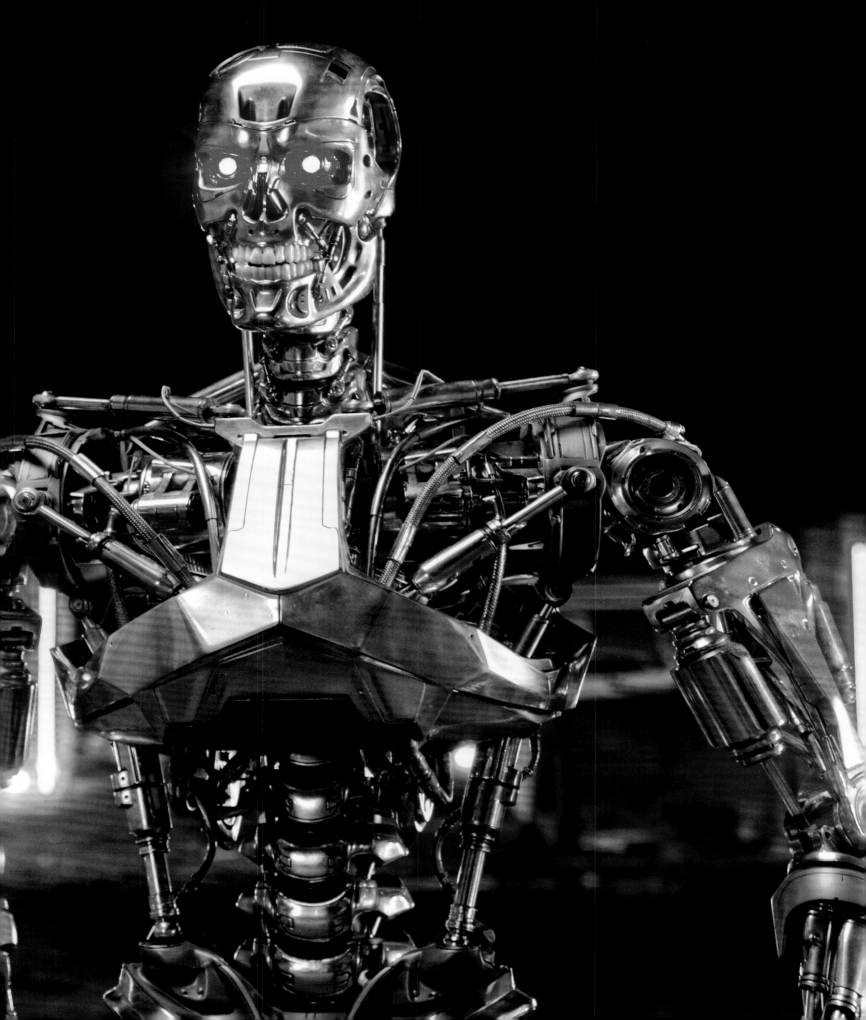

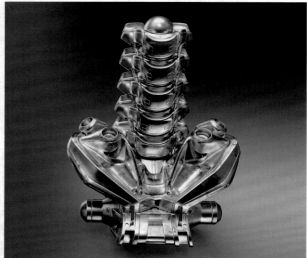

hand-crafted and molded and assembled. So it's still a very hands-on, intricate art that we do."

Legacy also built a key T-800 prop: the deactivated T-800, complete with gaping head wound, that Guardian lugs around after the Observatory sequence. Legacy used its life casts of Schwarzenegger from the '80s, as well as photos taken for the original movie, and so was able to mold an eerily accurate replica of his body and paint it to resemble him. "It's a pretty convincing piece," says Rosengrant. "That was a lot of work, but it gets a lot of screen time."

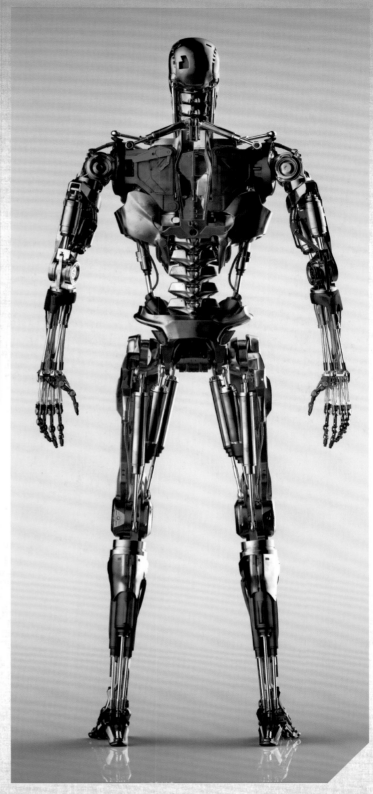

OPPOSITE TOP LEFT AND BOTTOM LEFT: Concept art for T-800 endoskeletons in action. OPPOSITE TOP RIGHT: A profile view of the redesigned T-800. OPPOSITE BOTTOM RIGHT: A digital render of the T-800's spinal chord and pelvis. ABOVE: Concept art showcases the redesigned endoskeleton.

T-1000

The liquid metal T-1000 is another iconic design that is getting an upgrade. Digital liquid simulations are far more sophisticated now than when *T2* was in production and Industrial Light & Magic was creating the then-revolutionary T-1000.

Peter Bebb of Double Negative feels that there should be a coherent design philosophy underlying all the cyborgs. "We kind of refer to that as the Cyberdyne design methodology," he says, "so we are not designing on a per-shot basis, and none of the technology that we are using is just made up. It has to have something that runs all the way through."

For the T-1000's upgrade, Sirrs and his team were looking at natural mimics such as cuttlefish and chameleons and studying exactly how they change their pigmentation. "When [T-1000 actor] Robert Patrick changed between his silver version and his human version, they just sort of faded

his color away. But we wanted to do something a bit more interesting than that," he says. Not only will the T-1000 change at a microscopic level, it'll go through secondary and tertiary phases when it changes form until it finally settles into the shape of Byung-hun Lee's L.A. cop.

Alan Taylor says Lee's physical performance as the dying T-1000 was one of the things he enjoyed most in the film. Lee says, "I tried to show that the machine was breaking down. I tried to show in that moment every emotion at the same time, i.e., suffering, sadness, happiness, rage, etc., as this powerful machine is destroyed." The director was impressed: "In the choreography he created," says Taylor, "he was doing things with his body I couldn't do without seriously hurting myself. It winds up being sort of ghastly and scary but sort of beautiful at the same time."

ABOVE LEFT: Concepts for the shape-shifting abilities of the T-1000 include hammer shapes as well as the classic "knives and stabbing weapons." ABOVE RIGHT: Putting accurate reflections on a mirror-like T-1000 is a significant VFX challenge. OPPOSITE BOTTOM LEFT: Full-body test renders of the T-1000. OPPOSITE BOTTOM RIGHT: A final frame of the deadly T-1000 in action.

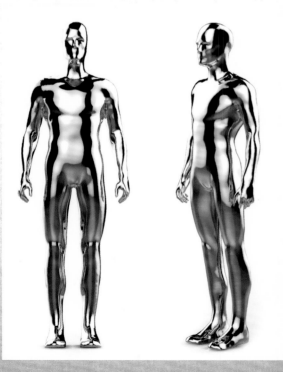

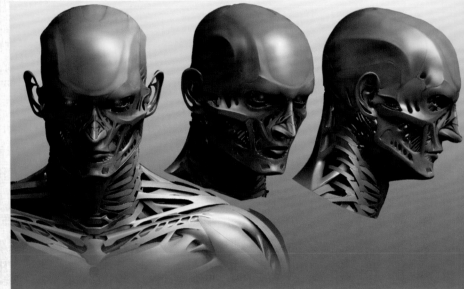

T-3000

The mandate for creating the new T-3000 that would take over the mind and body of John Connor and serve as the story's main antagonist was to create an iconic character built with nanotechnology that didn't look like anything in any other film. Sirrs told Peter Bebb that if the T-3000 didn't crash the "render farm"—the rooms full of servers that turn staggeringly complex digital files into VFX images—he hadn't done his job properly. It wasn't entirely a joke. Says David Ellison, "It has to be that way. If we're not pushing the technology to its breaking point, we're not fulfilling what Terminator movies promise an audience, which is groundbreaking visual effects."

It took thoughtful work to create that design. As with any creature, the visual effects artists started with the film's script: What's the T-3000's motivation, they asked, and what are its weaknesses?

They felt the T-3000's character was like a dark doppelgänger of human John Connor. "If John is the unquestioned leader of the resistance, T-3000 wants to become all-powerful," explains Hanson. "But his Achilles' heel is magnetic energy. And so we designed off of that, looking at how magnetism and magnetic energy work in the world naturally and in technology. That was all in the reference we pulled; for example, ferrous fluids, iron

TOP: Designs for the T-3000 reveal the creative thinking in visual effects. This terminator's look had to be new and instantly menacing. OPPOSITE: VFX renders show the T-3000 during visual development; note the sharp edges on one design and zombie-like anatomical details revealed in others.

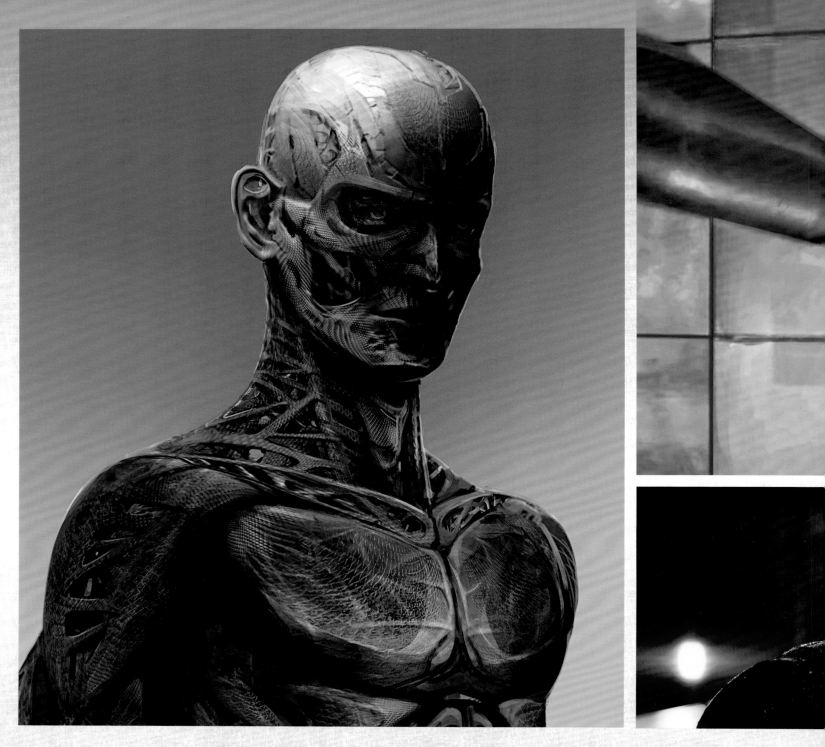

ABOVE: A more complete concept for the T-3000 shows the dark union of man and machine. TOP RIGHT: Concept art shows the T-3000 in the climactic battle from *Terminator Genisys*. OPPOSITE BOTTOM RIGHT: A painful-looking concept shows the nanotechnology fusing itself to a human skeleton. OPPOSITE BOTTOM LEFT: A final frame from *Terminator Genysis* shows the T-3000 in all its terrifying glory.

filings, and how sound travels through magnetic energy." They compiled a "mood reel" of such clips to find the textures and shapes that would define the new terminator. Then those were handed off to designers.

"We ended up asking ourselves, how would a computer actually design a human?" says Peter Bebb. "How could it improve upon it?" The first improvement: materials. Bebb sees it as a hybrid of T-800 and T-1000 technology, adopting the best of both. But where those models are robots without emotions as we understand the concept, the T-3000 blurs the line between mechanism and life form. "It's emotive," says Bebb. "It can get angry. It can react to certain situations. It's not just a machine. It's actually a living, breathing synthetic organism."

The T-3000's nanotech structure proved a puzzle, too. "As soon as you get into particulates, you get into something that can look like characters from other movies. It can almost look dusty and smoky, and we didn't want to get into that type of thing. So, if its weakness is magnetic fields and that's the thing that binds him as well, you can consider him like a pole.

He controls all of his form through being a very strong magnetic field." Among the inspirations for the design are frictionless, super-cooled Bose-Einstein fluids that form eerie ripples and patterns that look almost like a strange life form.

Sirrs uses the language of fractals to describe the T-3000: "Every part of him is a whole," he says. "We see him strip down to almost the individual particles at some point. So we are not just talking about the exterior appearance of this character." The T-3000's nature is most apparent when he fights Guardian in a hospital scene. The fight moves into an MRI machine, and when the machine's powerful electromagnets are turned on, the bonds holding the T-3000's nanoparticles together are overwhelmed. "We're trying to combine the sounds of an MRI into the actual design of the shot," says Bebb. "So it was almost design by sound, funnily enough, which is a kind of new concept. Everything we do is based off the sound design they give us, and then they can almost art-direct the shot from their perspective as well. We thought it was quite cool."

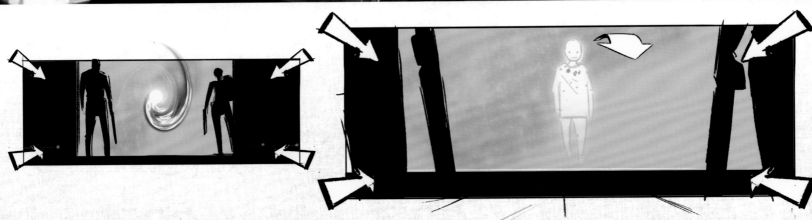

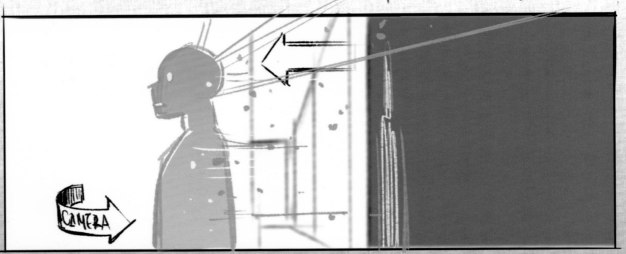

TOP: Concept art depicts the dramatic finale at Cyberdyne headquarters and the appearance of the T-5000 or "Skychild." ABOVE AND RIGHT: Storyboards show the first appearance of the Skychild, the holographic manifestation of Skynet's consciousness. OPPOSITE TOP LEFT: Concept art details a variety of Skychild looks. OPPOSITE TOP RIGHT: A final frame shows Skychild as it appears in *Terminator Genisys*. OPPOSITE BOTTOM: Concept art was used to nail down the final look of Skychild.

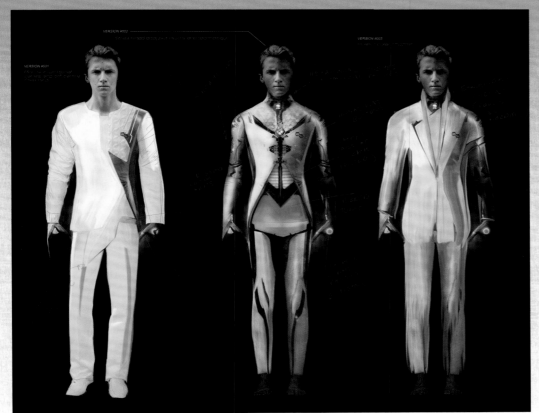

T-5000/SKYCHILD/SKYNET

The T-3000 is dangerous, but the greatest threat to humanity remains Skynet. But, like other devils, Skynet can assume a pleasing shape—or, at least, a human one.

Design-wise, the T-5000 is meant to convey rapid evolution, as "Genisys" comes online and the machine's consciousness is born. What better way to convey fast change than through the growth and development of a baby? The T-5000 begins as "SkyChild" but in minutes matures into none other than Matt Smith, the former *Doctor Who* star who appeared briefly in the 2029 scenes.

Again, the visual development of the T-5000 brought in a dizzying array of sources for inspiration. "It represents a birth," says Hanson. "We started throwing stuff together, and you end up with little plants popping out of the ground to the birth of a star. Hubble photography. We'll throw in holograms." Since it is literally a being of light with aspirations to godhood, religious images found their way into the mix, especially images of angels. Says Sirrs, "We wanted to instill this thing with an ever-increasing digital resolution and some sense of organic life. Resolution is not just a number of pixels; it's complexity."

On top of all that, Sirrs sought to add some kind of pseudoscientific underpinning to the T-5000, so that its appearance hints at the tech Skynet is using to project

itself: "It's not just a perfectly glowing figure made of light, because that almost appears magical."

Ellison sums up the whole effort succinctly: "There are many things that are large and spectacular in this movie—technologies and effects that require a tremendous amount of R&D—that nobody's ever seen before, and those will be cooking and baking and shifting up until the moment we deliver the movie."

18

CONCLUSION
(A LOOK AHEAD)

THE ENDING OF *TERMINATOR GENISYS* doesn't tie up every loose end—and since it's meant to launch a trilogy, that was never the intention. Writer Laeta Kalogridis says, "From our perspective, the most interesting thing about being able to plan it as three movies is that there are things that you can seed in the first movie that you know you're going to be able to do in the second and third." Ellison adds, "Skynet is a great example of that. In *Terminator Genisys* you're essentially seeing the birth of Skynet, but it will evolve to become an even more pivotal aspect of movies two and three."

Kalogridis offers this clue about what's to come: "The concept that souls will find each other, no matter what, is a huge part of what we're trying to do here. That no matter what happens they are drawn to each other. I'm a sucker for the idea of true love."

> ## "FROM OUR PERSPECTIVE, THE MOST INTERESTING THING ABOUT BEING ABLE TO PLAN IT AS THREE MOVIES IS THAT THERE ARE THINGS THAT YOU CAN SEED IN THE FIRST MOVIE THAT YOU KNOW YOU'RE GOING TO BE ABLE TO DO IN THE SECOND AND THIRD."

There are numerous unsolved mysteries in *Terminator Genisys*. The machines can't invent time travel, says Kalogridis, so who does and why? That will be addressed in the second film. Who sent Guardian back? Who programmed him to protect Sarah? And in this new version of the timeline, what does the future hold? Says writer Patrick Lussier: "If John Connor was not the savior of humanity and didn't exist, what would happen to the future? What shape would it take? Would somebody else rise up instead, or would there be no one? Would machine intelligence literally overrun everything?" And in the present or the very near future, when Skynet is awakening, will humanity fight back, or will people line up to purchase the same technology that will ultimately doom them?

Kalogridis is also looking forward to exploring an idea from Isaac Asimov and other classic science fiction writers: the tension between the momentum of time and the power of vast historical forces on the one hand versus the power of a single individual to shape

RIGHT: How human can a machine become? That's a question Arnold Schwarzenegger's performance as Guardian will explore in *Terminator Genisys* and its two planned sequels.

ABOVE: Concept art shows Sarah and Kyle in the 1984 Time Displacement Device preparing to be transported to 2017. OPPOSITE BOTTOM: A final frame from the film shows the TDD in action.

history on the other. An individual can stop such forces, she says, but "it's like damming a river. The amount of power required, the amount of sacrifice it takes, is massive. I think that's part of what we're trying to say. Things don't change easily. Things don't change without huge amounts of pain and loss."

Yet on the other hand, she says, a single person can change history. "What is the world without Alexander the Great?" she muses. "Well, it's not this world. That one individual is completely pivotal to current society. So there is a push and pull to the storytelling that I think the next two movies are going to focus on."

In keeping with the notion that there's "no fate but what we make for ourselves," Ellison and his team have mapped out a whole new future for the Terminator universe, and each of the individual characters will have their part to play. "Everything will tie together," he says. "Sarah, Kyle, Guardian—all of their stories are completely arced out. We can tell you what the last shot of the third movie is right now."

But where would the fun be in that?